God Called…

By Hank Leo Jr.

For Father Mike, Pastor Chris, Pastor Randy, Pastor Jeff, and my spiritual team in the "Wednesday Morning Club"...

Acknowledgements

First, and foremost, I would like to thank God, for giving me so many special moments throughout my life, and the courage and strength to write about and share them with others. I would like to thank my good friend, educator, and editor Debra Longnecker for her wonderful skills and time, as well as her support. I feel like I've assembled a very strong "spiritual team" consisting of Pastor Chris Kinnell, Pastor Randy Phillips, and Pastor Jeff Leahey, whom I lean on regularly to ask questions, guide, and steer me along my journey. And, most recently I've learned some important life lessons from our family's lifelong friend, Father Michael Carmola. Thank you all so much for showing me the light along my journey. *The Oneida Dispatch* has been wonderfully kind to allow me to share stories, thoughts, and anecdotes with the community through my weekly column. Thank you to the YMCA board, especially my brothers Matt Brown, John Elberson, Craig Bailey and Jeff Rowlands, members, and incredible staff for all of your support.

Thank you to the Wednesday morning basketball guys, for years of wonderful camaraderie and closing prayers. Much appreciation to our Wednesday Bible Study group at the Y for both your kindness and care. I'm sorry I have so many questions.

Thank you to my fellow riders in the Ride For Missing Children for giving me the chance to be a part of something truly special. I would especially like to thank my incredible Mom, Diane Leo, for her strength, and my Dad, Hank Leo Sr., for his continuous inspiration and my sisters Debbie, Sandy, and Terri, for being the greatest family a guy could have. Thank you to those friends who have stuck by me, through some tough times. John, Don, Mitch, Phil, Scott, Tom...you continue to surprise me with unconditional love and support. Lastly, thank you to my better half, Pauline, my biggest cheerleader and best friend.

COMMENTARY

"Reading the book God Called, I felt privileged to be allowed into a heart that has been touched by God. This book is both Hank's search for God and God's search for Hank. The author invites us to share the journey of his soul. One can only marvel at this love story between God and Hank, which flows into the lives of so many others. As the pages unfold, we witness the Word of God enter his head and then into his heart.

As I read these pages, they touched my heart. As he shared his experience, tears came to my eyes as I could only marvel at this love affair between God and Hank. Over and over again, as he shares his story, he concludes it with the phrase "God Called."

I especially appreciated his references to his parents. Having shared the journey of our youth with them through our school days, I know how blessed he was to be able to share the warmth and values of Hank Sr. and Diane. Certainly, he learned and experienced true love that reflects the One Great Love.

So many people today are searching for peace and inner joy. My prayer is that as many as possible will have the opportunity to enter into Hank's story and experience "God Calling" in their lives. Hank speaks for all of us when he says, "I was looking for answers to a lot of things; I was looking for peace." Our culture tells us that power, possessions, prestige, paychecks and promotions will give us that peace. Again, he describes it so well, when he says, "What used to be a life of selfish-focus has turned into a life of giving, helping and being alive."

It is my prayer that the journey of a soul will fall into the hands and hearts of so many who are trying so hard to discover what Hank has found and shared. Reading these pages will make you smile, cry and be filled with awe at the workings of God's spirit in one person's life. It can happen to each of us".

Rev. Michael J. Carmola

"Much of my time as a pastor is spent counseling, and working with others going through struggles in their lives. Some challenges seem small and some quite large, but I find they all have a few things in common.

One of these things is that they feel all alone. They feel isolated. So many people feel like they may be the only one dealing with a certain situation and they withdraw to lonely, dark places. As I listen and spend time with people, I have found we actually have a lot more in common than we think. Many of us get up in the morning putting on our happy faces. When our friends or co-workers ask how we are doing we say things like, "Things are going great;" or, " I am blessed." We don't want people to see our real struggles or our pain. We don't want people to know that we have weaknesses. We don't want to be vulnerable. The whole time we are lying to ourselves and showing others we have no struggle, when in reality we do.

Another common thing many people seem to deal with is their struggle to connect with God. They want to connect with him. There is something deep inside that knows there is a God. They sense a need for him, but they are too afraid to ask those questions or open up. Many people feel like God is mad at them or they have done too many bad things to ever find God working in their lives.

I love this book, "God Called" because Hank opens up and lets everyone see his struggle. Despite challenges and some really hard times, God was there through it all calling out to him. It was amazing to see the wonderful people God put in Hank's path. God put Hank in situations, and laid them out for him to behold. Things that may have seemed just a coincidence later proved to be a plan, and a very deliberate one. With this, God was calling Hank to His side.

I have been a Christian for a long time. I have been in the ministry for twenty years. I know that God has a plan for me. I have seen it time and time again. However, as I read this book I felt my confidence go to another level. I felt my hunger for God growing stronger. As I read, I saw some similarities in some struggles I have had in my past. I started to look at the challenges I have now differently. I started looking to my future with a renewed strength. If God had been reaching out to Hank in his struggle, I know he could be reaching out to me. I am not alone. God is calling out to me and working on my behalf.

As you begin to read this book, get ready to see God do amazing things within a humble man who just wanted to connect with his creator. Allow God to speak to you through Hank's story.   Realize nothing is by coincidence. God really does have a plan for your life. Just as God sent the right people at the right time into Hanks' life to guide him, God can do the same for you.   Just like God used some hard times and tough circumstances in Hank's life to call out to him, God can do the same for you. Be encouraged and know we are all "God Called"."

Pastor Jeff Leahey, Church On The Rock, Oneida, NY

"I have had the privilege of knowing Hank for several years. Most of that time was spent on the basketball court. But more recently, we meet on Friday mornings over breakfast and coffee to talk about important things, actually God things.

Hank asked me to read his new book, "God Called", and to share my thoughts about it. As a pastor, I found the book to be a wonderful read because it shared some life stories that we all grew up with. We all had church experience of some kind, some profound, some not so much.

What captured me most was that it showed Hank's journey with God. The stories he shares are funny, real, heart- wrenching, and personal. He has made the connection that much of life's experience can be God- ordained. And how we respond to those experiences can determine the level and intensity of the next encounter.

We all have a choice to react to life any way we wish. This book is a great story of growth - not physical growth, but rather, spiritual. Hank shares accounts of how he responded to God's calls and how those experiences have changed him. I am a witness to that change.

As a pastor and friend, it is exciting to see how Hank continues to respond to God's call. His mission is now, and has always been, to help people. It shows up in both his professional and personal life. After reading this account and working alongside Hank, I almost feel that I have become part of his book and his adventure.

I hope you enjoy reading this true, meaningful story, and just maybe, you too may note times in your life when God has called."

Pastor Randy Phillips
New Beginnings Community Church

REVELATION

There's an old joke about a man who sat on his rooftop during a great flood. As the waters were rising, a man in a boat came by and said, "Sir, get in," and the man on the roof replied, "No, that's okay; I'm praying and waiting for God to save me." Next, a lifeguard swam up to the house. The man refused his help and explained, "No, thank you; I'm waiting and praying for God to come and save me." Finally, a team of rescuers arrived in a helicopter, landing on the roof. One called to the man, "Sir, get in; the waters are rising and you will drown." The man replied, "I will not drown. I'm praying to God and asking Him to save me." The man eventually died in the waters as the flood took over his house. Upon arrival in heaven, the man asked God, "Why didn't you save me, Lord?" God replied, "Who do you think sent the boat, the lifeguard, and the rescue team?"

My spiritual journey has been somewhat like this old, dusty parable. As odd as it might seem, it took me many years to understand that God was calling me over and over again and I just wasn't listening or paying attention. Too many times God had offered me His help – a boat, a lifeguard, a whole rescue team – and too often I had misinterpreted or downright ignored His call.

Friends, family, even acquaintances might respond to this memoir by saying, "Since when did Hank become so religious? When did he ever read the Bible? What happened? What's all this God stuff?"

The truth is that I've always believed in God. But, I haven't always *participated* in Him. Even more importantly, *how* I got to this point, is not as important as *why*. What I do know is that it took me a long time to figure it out and this is the story of that process and the incredible results. I also know that I am still learning, still growing, and still developing. I don't push what I believe on others, nor do I judge them for what they believe. I'm not an authority figure or an expert on spiritual journeys; I'm not sure anyone is. All I can do is use what I've learned, try to make sense of it, and try to help others.

If people reading about my gift are inspired to head out on their own looking for their own signposts, I would be very comforted to think that a spark may have been ignited by a word, phrase, or experience that I am sharing. I am not alone in experiencing journeys with God. We all do. It was, in fact, the plan from the beginning. He's been calling us ever since we were old enough to hear. Little miracles are all around us and happen every day. Like the fellow in the old "rescue" joke, we just need to pay attention when He calls us.

I think my entire journey can be summed up by understanding that God has said to me, over and over again, "I told you so." The best part about the journey is that it is never too late to pay attention. It is never too late to apologize, and it is never too late to ask for forgiveness. It also doesn't matter to me that it took nearly fifty years to catch on. What matters most is that I do now.

The key question that I ask myself daily is "Why?" I think I've finally figured it out. On one hand, I'm not special. I am not a member of the clergy. I don't go to church every Sunday. I've been weak. I've made mistakes. I have hurt others. On the other hand, I'm as special as anyone else and know that God created me. Why wouldn't He call me to Him? I've felt like a lost sheep hundreds of times. I always wanted to be found. I know I will be tempted and tested along the way. But just as my good friend Pastor Randy said to me recently, "Don't let those times turn you away. It's the exact time you need to focus. Never give up on Him, and He won't give up on you."

Since the day the light bulb came on for me, I have had a craving for more knowledge, deeper understanding, and a yearning to share it with others. God has helped me help others. I believe that each one of us can be a shepherd to a lost soul. Even the toughest of cases is only an open hand away from being saved.

The more I read, learn, grow, and develop my relationship with God, the better my life becomes. I don't believe that's a coincidence. As I am faced with all kinds of questions, choices, and decisions at work, home, or in volunteer roles, I now feel like I have Someone in my corner. I find myself asking, "What do You want me to do?" and the direction becomes clearer. The only way I can describe it, is like when you are driving in a rainstorm and you turn on the windshield wipers and you can see the road clearly again, making you feel safer and more secure in your own abilities. Then, a rainbow comes out just over the horizon, followed by the warm sunlight shining brightly all around you. Hearing God's call has changed everything. Whether He sends a boat, a lifeguard, or a rescue team, the important thing is that I recognize His presence, hear His voice, and rely on His promise.

God called.

"Be strong and courageous. Do not fear or be in dread of them, for it is the LORD your God who goes with you. He will not leave you or forsake you" (Deut. 31:6).

CHAPTER 1

I sat in the fifth row from the back, to the right of the middle aisle, fiddling with my coat just before the 10:30AM service began at Christ Church. I hadn't been to church in quite a few weeks and felt like I needed to be there. Just a few rows ahead, a young boy, maybe nine or ten years old, was fiddling, too. He was whispering to people around him, squirming in his seat, half-standing up, then plunking down again. The next minute, he bumped his left leg against the old wooden pew and sat down with a slam. His dad, or grandpa, I couldn't be sure- grabbed his arm and pulled him down onto the seat and sternly reminded him, "You're in God's house, you know; sit still!" I could relate.

I remember being a little boy about this kid's age, being led to church by my mom, and dreading the hour-long "church school" before mass on Sundays. I actually thought "Shhh" was my name. Everyone in the seats behind me and in front of me called me that for a while. My mom and all the other neighborhood moms put us in a taxicab and had us "delivered" to the scary old church, where the not-so-nice, ruler-wielding ladies in weird blue superhero costumes battered us verbally into moral submission with commandments.

We took liberties with "Thou shall not kill" by trying to squish every ant and pull the wings off every fly we could find in the room. We also truly believed cats had nine lives and trying to end eight of them was a rite of passage.

I didn't mind the ride to church school. It was with Oscar the cab driver and we always tormented him by singing, "I wish I were an Oscar Meyer wiener" the whole way there and on the too-short ride home. I still feel for the guy because anybody willing to pack six or seven little hollering cherubs into a cab has got to have patience and a sense of humor. Looking back on it now, I find it hard to imagine a group of soccer moms packing their children into a city taxi, pooling a bunch of one dollar bills together, and saying, "Be off with them!" The child protective agencies would find them unfit for parental duty. But back in the early seventies, it was perfectly fine and worrying about safety was the last thing on anyone's mind. In fact, finding danger would have been much more fun than spending our Sunday mornings doing church things.

Oscar was a cigar-smoking, overweight, mound of a man who could have played Santa in a B-movie. He barely fit in the driver's seat and in those days there were no seatbelts. I'm not sure he would have been able to latch it, anyway. Most of the ride was spent with him looking in the broken, hanging-by-a-wire, rearview mirror, chomping on an unlit cigar. He joined right in on the lyrics, "And if I were an Oscar Meyer wiener, then everyone would be in love with me," emphasizing the *meeeeeee.* We thought the ride to church and back was the best part of the entire experience.

The nuns did their best to relate the story of the birth of Jesus to something we would understand, but we had so many questions, they just became more and more annoyed and frustrated.

> "Sister, if God created the earth, why did He leave a big hole in it called the Grand Canyon? I thought He was perfect."
>
> "Sister, if God created Adam and Eve, why would he put them in a garden?"
>
> "There's a Father, a Son, and a Holy Spirit that are all the same guy? The Father's son is Him? Why aren't the Father and Son holy too?"
>
> "Did God write the Bible? Because if he did, He should've written it in English."
>
> "How come God doesn't have to get a haircut and we do?"

The list went on and on.

After trying to explain things to us, they sent us away, stuffed us back into Oscar's cab, told us to come back next week, and gave us Chapters 1, 2, and 3 for homework. I don't recall Oscar ever wondering what we had learned about in church school, and I'm pretty sure he was not poised to serve as a role model or chaperone, supporting any of the directives drilled into us by the nuns. By the way the car swerved from left to right trying to avoid running over a dead squirrel or hitting a pothole on the rain-soaked streets, our safety seemed not to be his concern. Seven little kids pinned to the right-hand side of the Ford Granada yelling, "Get off me!" just made it all the more fun for us.

"How was church school, Hanky?" my mom always asked.

"Really cool; you should've seen the squirrel Oscar hit. Blood and guts everywhere!" I'd exclaim.

What I remember most about church school was reciting the Lord's Prayer. We really didn't try or want to know what it meant. You were just cool if you could recite it word for word and the sisters were impressed that you must have studied it, to be able to repeat it verbatim. I was one of those kids.

In church the following week, I would stand up when it was time, and after picking my underwear out of my seat, re-adjusting my clip-on tie, and making a few random bodily noises – I'd prove I was clearly as accomplished as all the rest of the people around me.

"Our father, who art in heaven..."

The adults would turn and smile politely, and I have to admit that I was quite proud of myself. "You've got a nice little Catholic boy there, Mrs. Leo," Mrs. Smith would say. I remember feeling bad that maybe God knew I was not really interested in listening to all these people echo what the old guy in the white robe up front was saying. I was more interested in the sounds and sights of the grand old church.

The dark, wooden closets that the old ladies with funny hats went into to whisper were scary. The clanking of the swinging gold locket with smoke coming out of it was bizarre. And the statues looking down on me seemed to be from the Middle Ages. They looked like gargoyles from old movies. I wondered how everyone seemed to know the songs and knew ahead of time which page they were going to be on in the big red book. I also couldn't figure out why they all knew the tunes. I reasoned that everyone in church must have taken music lessons and could read the notes on the page. I lip-synched words that I made up to make people think I knew them. I didn't. I was out of tune, both musically and spiritually.

Time seemed to crawl and because there were no clocks in sight, it seemed like forever. When the priest mentioned that if we believed in God, we could live for eternity, I was thinking that he was referring to the length of the mass. I would usually end up having a laughing fit, where I just couldn't stop, or I'd make sounds that would echo throughout the whole sanctuary. On would come the "Shhhh's."

When it was time for communion, I was just plain nervous. I wasn't sure what to say when the priest put the white, flat, tasteless wafer on my tongue and held a gold platter under my jaw. I assumed it was there in case there were crumbs or it missed my mouth. I assumed he knew how sloppy I was when I ate and didn't want me to go home with stuff all over my shirt. I also wanted to try the wine. I couldn't figure out why so many people went through the wine line yet there was always some left over. It was like an endless fountain that never had to be refilled. I had heard the phrase, "My cup runneth over," and thought this experience was where it came from. I always took the host and kept it on my tongue as I walked all the way to the back, my head down, hoping I'd performed the whole ceremony correctly. I remember being told I was eating the "body of Christ," and that confused and scared me.

There didn't seem to be anyone responsible for correcting me and telling me that the way I was doing it was wrong. I just kept walking to my seat, usually forgetting exactly where it was, and wondering how my row would switch to accompany the change in directions when I finally found it. I used to count the huge white columns to remember where I was. When I found my aisle, I'd turn my knees sideways and shimmy along the pew, balancing on the kneeling pad, saying, "Excuse me" dozens of times. I felt badly that people had to get up from their knees while praying to let me through.

During mass, we would stand, then sit, then stand, then kneel. I never knew which one it was going to be or how everyone knew. I just followed along, much like everything else I did in church. It was frightening, overwhelming, and most of my attention was paid scanning the ceiling, looking at the massive paintings, incredible architecture, and watching who was coming in late. If I saw someone I knew, I would smile and look down.

The church choir was always really together in their harmonies, but there was also this high-pitched squealing vibrato of a voice that always shrieked above the others. You could never see the choir because they were up above and behind us, and I sat so far in the back, that looking up meant looking at the floor above me. I thought to myself, "Maybe they put her up there for a reason." I used to try to block out the whole choir, and listen just to that one high-pitched voice. It was like trying to hone in on Art Garfunkel. Whatever the message was, I didn't hear it.

It always seemed as if the priest was an old guy, being stern with me. It seemed like he was telling the crowd not to do stuff, not to say this, not to say that, not to be like this, not to look at things this way or that way. And he seemed to know what he was talking about and everyone listened. I heard "Amen" frequently and took that to mean everyone agreed with him, even though they were being scolded. I would try to follow along in the book, but he sang some of the words in a very monotone and nasal voice, trying to get through a passage. I felt bad for him. I wondered who made him sing those parts.

I felt lost and not sure if this was right for me. I had plenty of questions and one of them was for myself. "Am I supposed to be here?" There never was a reply. There wasn't some lightning bolt that came down from heaven. There wasn't any whisper in my ear, no booming voice from above. Nothing. I just didn't know. I wasn't sure what this was all about or what I was supposed to be doing. The scary part was, I wasn't sure if anyone else knew, either.

God called.

"but Jesus said, 'Let the little children come to me and do not hinder them, for to such belongs the kingdom of heaven'" *(Matt.19:14).*

CHAPTER 2

I stopped going to church for a lot of years. Of course I went for a wedding if I had to, or a funeral if I was made to. But on any given Sunday, I had better things to do.

It wasn't until my early twenties that I decided to give it another try. This time, I was really going to try to pay attention and do what I had always done- think, reason, figure it out, make sense of it. I started by trying to say a little prayer when I received communion: "Please God, let this give me the strength to be a good person, and help me. I'm not sure where I want to work or live, so make it quick." I'd usually follow it with, "Please!" I figured God would listen more carefully to prayers that reflected good manners. Whenever I prayed, I'd try to say them in the language I was used to hearing in church. It made sense to me that if I said prayers in my head using big, religious words, God would pay more attention to them. "Father almighty, maker of all seen and unseen, please taketh my prayers and guideth me toward a life filled with abundance and happiness."

I had no idea what I was saying. And I was convinced He didn't either. I was selfish. I wanted to ask for help with whatever it was that was bothering me. If a girlfriend broke up with me, I prayed she would come back. If my dog got sick, I'd pray he wouldn't die. The prayers were always issued to help *me.*

I started questioning things and wondering about topics I should have pursued when I was younger. I felt it was okay to ask them now because probably God hadn't heard me in the past. I wasn't sure about all of the standing up, sitting down, kneeling, singing, repeating things just to repeat them. I felt inadequate to be in church when those around me seemed to "get" it. I usually sat alone, and if someone came to sit in the pew near me, I would slide down and leave a gap. I remember hearing that we needed to confess our sins, and I thought of the times I put hot sauce on my sister's peanut butter and jelly sandwich. I didn't understand or believe that you just had to ask for forgiveness and your slate was clean, leaving room for you to make even more mistakes. It didn't seem right. But neither did life.

I call my twenties the "Blackout Period." I don't think I paid attention to much. I kind of just worked, played, and went home. Everything was temporary. Not much was important. I've always been an observer, someone who sees and hears things to learn. I'm terrible at reading directions and I'm much better when someone shows me, rather than tells me what or how to do something. From what I learned in church and church school, religion seemed like a bunch of rituals without much meaning and without any impact on me. As I grew older, I felt guilty for not having paid attention when I was younger and I felt like I needed someone to talk to, someone to help me figure out if I was headed down the right path or the wrong one.

I was always what I would call a good person. I cared about others, going out of my way to help when there was a need. In fact, I remember praying one time to let me save someone's life. But I kind of just went through the motions of living. I couldn't understand why bad things happened to good people and why bad people got away with doing bad things. Nothing seemed to make sense.

I spent a great number of years avoiding church and avoiding God. Whenever I heard someone quote scripture, I wrote them off as a fanatic. I often doubted that they knew what they were talking about.

It wasn't until I was in my early thirties that I met a graduate student, Jen, majoring in theology. She seemed very happy, very secure, and very sure of her feelings. She believed in God and I would overhear her sharing stories with others. It piqued my interest and I began talking to her. That's when things started to change. I wasn't sure if it was too late to make amends with God, to apologize for not listening, to ask for forgiveness for ignoring the meaning behind the rituals. I decided to give it a try, expose my ignorance, and talk.

At first, it was just casual. "So, you study the Bible? That's pretty cool. What do you want to be, a nun?" I asked. I recalled my childhood memories of Sisters Agnes, Josephine, and Gertrude and I hoped this young lady was not going to turn out that way.

"No, Hank, I want to be a chemistry teacher," she replied.

"Chemistry?" I asked, with two raised eyebrows.

"Yeah. After I get home from Zimbabwe, I'll finish my second major," she said with confidence.

When asked why she would be going to a far-off country, she explained that she was part of a team that was taking water, food, and supplies to a tribe that had next to nothing. I wondered why anyone would take time away from work to volunteer to go to a third world country, but she seemed genuinely happy. And I was curiously jealous.

After a few weeks of talking, I asked Jen if it would be okay if I asked her a few questions that had been on my mind for years, but had been too afraid to ask. She was several years younger than I, and I was risking sounding like an idiot, or at least someone who should have known these things from "church school."

"Who wrote the Bible?"

Jen replied, "Well, it was written by a lot of people."

I elaborated, "I don't understand 'The Book of Joshua' and 'The Book of Isaiah.' Are these books or is the Bible the book? I'm confused."

She responded, "It took a lot of work, research, approval systems, and processes for the accounts of Christ to be included in the Bible."

My response was, "But doesn't it say in THE Bible that God created earth? So who would have seen him do that and who wrote it down to prove it?"

I felt like a little kid questioning the existence of the tooth fairy, and I felt ignorant that I was asking questions that were so simple. But I was excited, and wanted to learn more. She was patient with me. "You're trainable, Hank. You just came up with the entire reason faith exists."

I was confused, because I wasn't sure that I had come up with anything other than question marks. She handed me a few verses to read in a study Bible. "You can borrow mine. Read."

she said. She gave me dozens of verses to look up and started calling me throughout the days ahead to hear what I thought about them.

That first night, I took out the book she had given me and flipped to the verses she'd written down. They were mostly from the Psalms. I wondered why she didn't ask me to start reading the Bible from the beginning, as I would do with any book.

I sent her an email inquiring just that.

She emailed back: "There's an Old Testament and a New Testament. You'll find the New much more interesting. Just give the ones I highlighted a try and we'll talk tomorrow."

The next evening, I saw Jen and she could sense my excitement. "What did you think of the verse?" she asked. Of course, the one she asked about was one of the only ones I hadn't read. I was embarrassed and said, "I really like the Psalms. They're like little life lessons."

Jen responded, "I like those, too. But don't forget the others, okay?" I was beginning to feel comfortable at her lack of judging me, and I was surprised at my new ability to open up and share.

It was new and refreshing. I was beginning to feel special, accepted, and worth saving. And, I was reading again.

I was nervous that I was heading toward religion, and what people might think of me. I would hear people whom I thought were connected to God say things like, "I feel blessed" and they would quote Scriptures. I wondered if they really knew what they were saying and what the words meant. I also wondered if they really believed the things they were saying or if they were saying them to make others believe they were religious and therefore more righteous than they were.

I didn't want to be one of them. Instead, I wanted to learn. And the first lesson was not to judge them and instead, worry about me. "Jen, can we go back to the whole history thing again?" I asked.

"Sure, what are you thinking about?" she responded.

I proceeded to bombard her with questions about the authenticity of the Scriptures. Who wrote the Bible? Were the stories literal or metaphorical? Where is the Arc? Would dinosaurs have been on it? Every answer seemed to spur a new question.

Patiently, Jen explained as best she could. "The beginning of the book is about God setting up life for us, giving us the rules. It's a bit dry, but important. The real stuff is in the New Testament. That's where you learn the themes, the mission, the beauty of the Scriptures. It's where God appeals to us as a real person."

I liked hearing that. But my inquisitive mind and my anal retentiveness told me to start from the beginning, read everything, and try to learn. When I told Jen this, she said, "Well, I guess if you want to, but it's the long way around." Typical. I usually do take the long way around in things. "In the beginning, God created the heavens and the earth..."

Life went on for a while. I thought about what Jen had said, and about how I felt. I wasn't really reading many books at the time, only headlines in the newspaper. I was watching the news on television once in a while, but little else. Basically I was just existing and aging. I was also becoming disgruntled with all of the bad news I read daily, including terrorism, murder, child pornography, theft, and more. I was also working several jobs, volunteering at several places, and in and out of relationships. I was always wondering what was wrong with the other person, trying to figure out why she'd left, or why I'd left, or why I couldn't commit to something - anything. I also hadn't been to church in a while. Life was okay. I knew I was a good person. But

I felt empty, alone, uncommitted to anything – while committed to everything – if you know what I mean. I didn't like myself and I was insecure. And, being alone was one of my favorite things to do. There had to be something better.

God called.

"Whoever isolates himself seeks his own desire; he breaks out against all sound judgment" (Proverbs 18:1).

CHAPTER 3

Time passed, and although I began getting caught up in work, I kept thinking about God and learning more about Him, who He was, and what I needed to do. I kept thinking that maybe I needed to take more time to reflect and explore my beliefs. I actually said to myself, "Pay attention, Hank. Pay attention. Stop going from place to place, from work, to home, to the store, to wherever, without looking around you. Stop and pay attention. You are missing out." I actually started thinking about death - no, not about suicide. On the contrary, I started thinking, "I'm getting older. I probably have a few more dozen Christmases. I probably have forty more birthdays. The way I'm eating, I might only have thirty.

I missed my nephew's birthday. I didn't say "Happy Anniversary" to my Mom and Dad in August. I couldn't remember what my sister's promotion was for. "What if today were my last day on earth?" I questioned. "Did I do enough? Was I selfish? What would my legacy be? Am I good enough to go to heaven, or am I going to hell?" I felt guilty. I felt alone. I felt inadequate. I remembered everyone I had wronged in some way, and I thought of how it must have made them feel. I thought of how selfish I could be at times and I wondered if I had enough time to make good on my poor choices. I wanted to apologize to them.

I'd never used the word "sin" before, but that's what these felt like. It was time to make some changes.

After work one night, I stopped at Barnes & Noble, one of my favorite places. Usually I would walk around and look at the latest sports magazine, trying to find some new story about my beloved New York Mets, God's last miracle. I would sit in one of those big, comfy chairs in the back and mostly look around at the people. I'd go check out the humor section and read cartoons, or thumb through biographies. The number of employees who had asked me, "Can I help you find anything?" numbered in the hundreds over time. I always responded with, "No thanks, I'm fine."

In reality, that was a lie. I *wasn't* fine and I *was* looking for something. I was looking for answers to *a lot* of things. Mostly, I was looking for peace. I'm a hyper person on the inside, though not many know that. I've always thought of myself as a duck - calm and cool on the outside and paddling like crazy underneath. Peace, for me, would have been the greatest gift I could ever get. And I found it at Barnes & Noble.

This particular night, I walked over to the *Religion and Christianity* section and decided to buy a Bible. There were so many versions; I didn't have any idea of which I should get. I literally chose the first one I saw, "NIV," not having a clue what that meant. When I read the acronym, I still didn't. The New International Version meant nothing to me. What I liked about it, though, was that the cover said, "With helps" and "Words of Christ in Red Letters." With a few doubts about all this, I opened to the first page.

The "About the Bible" listed a few paragraphs such as "What is the Bible?" and "How was the Bible Written?" and "How the Bible Came to Us." I thought to myself, *Finally, something that can explain all of the questions I might have, and it's in my hands.* I couldn't believe that I hadn't done this earlier. I felt pretty stupid. I also felt like I should have been taught all this before, but realized that maybe I had been, but had been focusing on other things, like Oscar the cab driver, and dead squirrels instead.

There it was, the world's most read and revered book, right in front of me. I am an intelligent, thoughtful guy who can read, write, and understand, but I'd never given this book a chance. I'd read Dr. Seuss, but not the Bible? In the past, the Bible was this massive, thin-paged, old-English collection of books that had words I could not understand, and an awful lot of people "got it" except for me. It was time.

When I got home that night, I started reading the first chapter, again. "In the beginning, God created the heavens and the earth." I wondered if God had really called the thing we live on "the earth" or if that was something some author wrote years later. I wondered about the early explorers who had thought the earth was flat. What would the authors of the Bible know about the earth?

Who quoted God if he was the first person alive? was my crazy line of thinking. I started feeling guilty that I was asking the same questions I had asked years ago. But this time was different. I had a guide, a goal, and I wanted to know. And, I thought that if the Bible was actually the truth, and God did in fact create the heavens and the earth that he certainly was able to listen to me and communicate with me.

"Jen...can I talk to you?"

"Of course, Hank, what can I help you with?"

"I'm lost." Silence. "Jen?"

"I'm here. And, yes, maybe you are."

"Um, okay, what do I do?"

"Learn to trust me."

"I do, Jen. Why?"

"I'm not there with you, Hank, right?"

"No, I'm at Barnes and Noble; of course not."

"You don't see me, right?"

"No, Jen."

"You want my help, right?"

"Of course. That's why I called."

"Do you believe I would help you if you asked?"
"Um. Yes, I do."

"You just defined God, Hank."

Things started to change for me after that conversation. I decided to give it a try. I knew it wasn't going to be easy, and I knew I'd have my doubts, but at least I understood that not everything had to be seen to be believed. And I understood that someone cared for and about me, yet didn't want anything in return, didn't have ulterior motives, and wasn't trying to get me to do anything for them. It was humbling, human, real, and special. It was like hearing my dad say, "Walk right here next to me; I'll protect you," as we walked out on the frozen lake to ice fish when I was ten. I was now armed with the belief that maybe there was good out there. And, it felt safe and warm.

In my mind, I started to realize that I had been wrong. Sitting on the floor in my living room, making a conscious effort to focus, pay attention, and believe, I closed my eyes. I asked myself, "What do you see?" After several moments of silence, the answer was *beauty*. It could have been death, murder, bicycling, snow tires, hairspray, or a car wash. I didn't see any of those things. I felt warm, whole, peaceful, and thankful. It was the first time I had experienced peace and recognized it. I thought of my mom and dad. I thought of my three great sisters. I thought of my friends. I thought of all I have. And, I was thankful. That night, lying down on my bed, I turned off the light. After a few seconds, I flipped on my light and took out my new Bible. I decided to open it, at about the middle, just a random spot, and see what I would stumble upon.

"Show me your ways, LORD,
teach me your paths.
Guide me in your truth and teach me,
for you are God my Savior,
and my hope is in you all day long.

Remember, LORD, your great mercy and love,
for they are from of old.
Do not remember the sins of my youth
and my rebellious ways;
according to your love remember me,
for you, LORD, are good" (Psalm 25: 4-7).

I thought to myself, *Isn't that appropriate for what I've been going through? What a coincidence.* Now that I look back on it, I realize that this was the first time God called. But it never struck me that it was by design or on purpose. I just thought it was luck, chance, happenstance or irony.

It wasn't.

God called.

CHAPTER 4

A smile came upon me. It was like I was being talked to, and listening intently for once. I actually recall being sad. I was sad that I hadn't seen it earlier.

Now that I was intentionally tuning in to hearing God's call, I became more sensitive to all kinds of sounds. I have always been a music fan. It's not so much the lyrics, the tune, the artist, or the singer. It's the way it makes me feel and the way it makes others feel. I like to see smiles and reactions. Music tends to do that to people. I like when I hear a song either in the car, in a store, or on the radio, and someone likes it and just starts dancing. Pulling up next to a VW Rabbit and hearing "Walking On Sunshine" with four ladies singing in almost harmony just makes me grin. Sometimes they do a little dance in the driver's seat, or bob their head, or flat out break dance in public. It's just one of those things that gives me peace. Music does this to me too, but I'm a bit of an oddball. I listen to Louis Armstrong, Miles Davis, Coleman Hawkins, and John Coltrane. When I'm in a great mood, I play New Orleans brass band music. And sometimes I do my happy dance - if no one is watching.

Back in 2003, I was able to write a grant for the YMCA that allowed me to bring in musicians from New Orleans after Hurricane Katrina. If you've ever been to New Orleans, you know the spirit of the music and the role it plays in the culture there. It is infectious and spiritual. The grant kind of took care of two of my greatest passions - helping kids and helping New Orleans. Both were in need at the time. Because we brought in some amazing New Orleans street musicians, I wanted to capture whatever I could, permanently.

We had a wonderful youth music program at the Y, with nearly 100 kids who were aspiring musicians themselves. We had an amazing instructor who cared deeply about them personally and musically. I wanted to contribute what I could and give them an experience in life they would never forget. I also wanted to share the gift of music, a gift that made me feel good, with others. It was a perfect opportunity. I am not a music producer, nor do I read music, perform it, or play an instrument. I can't carry a tune in a bucket. But, I knew what music could do.

After several performances, clinics, and concerts featuring the New Orleans musicians working with the Y kids on the project, I was able to connect with other nationally known artists to whom I'd been referred. At one of our performances in Rome, NY, one of our donors came up to me and said, "My husband's lifelong dream was to have the Harlem Boys Choir come to Rome, New York. He passed away before he ever realized his dream. Do you think you could get them to come here, Hank?" I told her I would look into it.

Later that day, I went back to my office and searched the Internet for the Harlem Boys Choir. They had recently become defunct after their founder Walter Turnbull had passed away. However, they had formed an alumni group and there was a contact name and number - "George Reyes." I called him.

George told me the group would, in fact, be interested in coming to Rome. The Harlem Boys Choir, or what used to be the Harlem Boys Choir, was now the Boys & Girls Choir of Harlem Alumni. It consisted of alumni of the original group. I still had funds available from the grant, so we booked the date and scheduled the bus ride and hotel rooms. I believed that this would be a nice opportunity to record the Choir with the Y kids. I really didn't have much of a plan for how to use the recording, only thinking that it would be good to have, if they would do so.

Over the years, several people had written and shared songs with the Choir and I suggested to George that we consider using some of them with the combined groups. After listening to about a dozen of them, I suggested "There is a Beacon in NY Harbor" and "Let Him Soar." I liked the feeling I got when I heard them. I didn't really know what they were about, who wrote them, or why. I liked the tunes, the lyrics, and the way they moved me. What I didn't realize at the time was that they were written by the same author, and I had picked them randomly.

As we were preparing for the world famous Choir to come to central New York, the kids in the music program were bubbling with excitement and so was I. George recommended that I get in touch with their arranger, Joel Martin. A quick conversation with Joel led me to understand he was a man of great depth, unquestionable musical knowledge, and a great sense of humor. "Hank, have you ever Googled your own name?" he asked on our first phone call. I confessed I hadn't, and he encouraged me to do so, saying it could be quite interesting. Later that week, I found out that my name was the name of a famous racing horse. I also found out Joel was an amazing man.

As the concert approached, we sent out press releases about the YMCA kids performing and recording with the amazing "Boys & Girls Choir of Harlem Alumni." The headline *Y to Record Two New Songs with Famous Choir* graced the local newspaper. We were all excited, and couldn't wait for the day to get here. We booked the theatre and started selling tickets. We reached out to PBS and asked them if there might be interest in covering the concert. There was.

Then, I received a phone call that I will never forget. Roy Schryver, an elementary music teacher in Connecticut, contacted me to say that years ago, he had sent two songs to the Harlem Boys Choir, hoping they would perform them. Having never heard back from them, Schryver assumed nothing would come of it until he read a press release about our upcoming performance.

What he was saying was that he and his colleagues had written "There Is A Beacon" AND "Let Him Soar." Schryver explained, "Originally, the song started out as 'There is a Beacon in Flanders School.' 'Let Him Soar' was about the school's founder, Walter Turnbull."

All this time, I had assumed that "There is a Beacon" was a tribute to 9/11. Schryver conceded that it could be interpreted as such, but the origins went back much further.

I decided on the spot that Roy and his colleagues needed to be at the show. He accepted and his enthusiasm was compounded when I explained that the performance would be recorded for PBS.

The day arrived. As the Choir was warming up, in the theatre appeared Roy Schryver, his beautiful wife Beverly, and the other writers. I escorted them to the rehearsal to watch and listen. We sat together. The Choir literally shook the room, the walls vibrating with the soaring highs and thundering lows. Then, out came the first line, "There is a beacon in New York Harbor," and we all cried. We knew the significance. We "got it." We marveled at the odd chance that the two worlds would come together. We knew it probably wasn't by fate, and it certainly wasn't by luck. For me to choose these two songs out of dozens, and for Roy to read the press release from hundreds of miles away, and for us to be sitting in the same theatre, listening to the amazing Boys & Girls Choir of Harlem Alumni singing a song that was written long ago, for an unspecified purpose - it was what some might have called "magic." It wasn't.

A few years later, after that unbelievable night, George and I were speaking about getting back together for another event. "How about on 9/11?" I asked. I had received something in the mail about a series of concerts being performed on that date as a part of a tribute to the victims. "Is the Choir available?" I asked. "There are concerts all over the city, Hank; it would be a great time. Let's do it," George responded. Many of the kids who performed in the original recording had since aged out of the program and moved on, so we recruited a number of new students, began rehearsing, and learned the songs all over again. "Up for round two, Maestro?" I asked Joel Martin excitedly on the phone. "Of course!" was the response.

It wasn't long before the kids were ready and we set out on a bus down to the Big Apple, with twenty-three young people, their parents, our staff, and a ton of pride. We arrived at the famous Jazz at Lincoln Center facility to rehearse once again with the Choir. Shortly after, we were on our way to the New York Public Library steps, the same steps the kids had seen in the movie *Ghostbusters*. When we arrived, the kids set up their instruments and the entire Choir came out of one city bus. It was 9/11; it was special; and we were there.

During warm ups, street crowds started to gather. Our ensemble was a large one. It is estimated that nearly 600 people stopped to see and hear the angelic choir perform "There is a Beacon in New York Harbor" and "Let Him Soar" with young children from upstate New York not too far from where the Twin Towers once stood. It was incredible. We filmed the performance that day and dedicated it to Terry Wright, the lead singer and director of the Choir, who had recently passed away.

The two songs and video can now be found in the National Archives at Ellis Island, a permanent part of the Archives. And since, the Choir has performed the song live for the President of France, showing America's appreciation for the gift of the Statue. It is now one of the official songs at the Statue of Liberty. God called.

"'For I know the plans I have for you,' declares the LORD, 'plans to prosper you and not to harm you, plans to give you hope and a future'"(Jeremiah 29:1).

CHAPTER 5

During this whole process, George suggested another singer for me to contact for our recording project. "Hank, how would you like to have the lead singer of the Marvelettes on your project?" George inquired.

"Are you kidding? Absolutely!" I said, eagerly wanting to find out more.

"I'll give her your number."

Denise Morgan called me the next week and after five minutes on the phone it seemed like I had known her my whole life. We laughed and shared stories. She was funny and engaging. I just loved her. "Do you have any ideas for a song you want to do with us?" I asked.

"Well, there is a song I wrote twenty-nine years ago, Hank. It's called "Where are They" and I never recorded it. Can I send it to you?" She asked.

"Please do. I'll let you know what we can do," I replied, beaming with excitement.

The package arrived a few days later at the Y. I opened it, and all that was in the envelope was a cassette tape. I didn't even own a cassette player anymore; in fact, I thought they were extinct. We asked an audiophile friend if he would convert it to a CD for us. He obliged.

The next day, I was driving to a meeting with the Community Foundation to talk about applying for a grant. I popped the CD into my player and listened to a song that would change my life.

Where are They?

I shed a tear tonight

Peacefully sleeping

Or living in fright

Where are the children?

Where are my children?

Tonight?

It was scratchy, rough, raw, and beautiful. A tear slowly dripped down my cheek as I tried to make it through and collect myself for the meeting.

What kind of mind could plan such a thing?

What kind of person, this misery would bring

How do they know

And not let go

Oh, where are they?[1]

---

[1] Morgan, Denise. *Hope Is In Me – A Musical Journey*, Rome, NY. 2010

To say I was overcome with something - not just the lyrics, but the tone, the feeling, and the emotion - was an understatement. I brought the CD into the meeting with me and asked the Director if she knew of anyone from the National Center for Missing & Exploited Children. She mentioned Kelli Corasanti's name and I asked her to bring her in so we could all listen to this recording.

Before Kelli arrived, I wondered if there was a way we could record the song with Denise and somehow incorporate NCMEC. When Kelli arrived, we brought out a CD player and played "Where are They?" for the group. We all either teared up or downright cried, and we knew we had something special, something moving, that was very powerful.

"The Ride for Missing Children is in a few weeks, Hank. Maybe this would work in the closing ceremony," Kelli suggested.

I got on it and after considering the logistics, I called Denise and shared with her the news that we wanted her to come and perform the song. The Ride for Missing Children is a fundraising tribute to children who are missing and the families that are looking for them. Five hundred bike riders pedal 100 miles to raise awareness and money for things such as posters that are used to publicize these cases.

Denise arrived in Rome, NY just about a week later and we began rehearsing the song. She was particular about how it should sound, and rightfully so. After many hours of work, we were ready, and so was she. The closing ceremony of the Ride is an experience for the ages. The 100 riders gathered in a large recreation center, surrounded by children who have been recovered, parents who are still looking, hundreds of volunteers, and supporters who care deeply about the cause.

The lights dimmed and white candles were lit and held by all of the riders. I came out to the podium and introduced Denise to the 2,500 or so in attendance. She delivered the most gut-wrenching, heart-stopping vocals while the kids accompanied her. She stopped several times to catch her breath and collect her emotions, but she made it through. A standing ovation followed. I'll never forget that day, the impact it had, and the words that echoed throughout the venue. It was as if the roof opened up and God said, "I hear you all, and I am with you."

After that performance, I vowed to have the Y take a lead role in the prevention of missing children and I began to work closely with volunteers from NCMEC. The Ride leaves early in the morning from the Oneida Troopers' barracks, where the Opening Ceremonies are held. That year, however, the barracks were under construction and organizers asked if I would consider hosting them at the Y, just up the hill. I never gave it a second thought. "We would be honored."

During a walk-through of the YMCA that day, in preparation for the upcoming event, Frank Williams, the Chairman of the Ride remarked politely, "Hank, why don't you ride with us this year?" It wasn't necessarily in the form of a question. Under my breath, I said to myself, *Hank, you haven't ridden a bike since you were twelve and it had three wheels. This is a hundred miles. You don't even have a bike and you're about thirty pounds overweight.* There was no way I was going to do this ride. "I would be honored to," is what left my mouth and what was heard by the entire committee, including Frank. They may have thought they were just getting Rider number 498. I knew better. Whenever I get involved in something, I give it my all.

I started taking spinning classes at the Y three nights a week and eventually bought a bike. I bought the cheapest one and remember asking the salesman at the store which one would be best for me. "Um, I'm doing this Ride in May, and I need a bike. What's the difference between this $10,000 one and the $400 one?" I asked stupidly.
"Well, you have to peddle both of them, so I guess it's up to the rider," he responded.

"I'll take the $400 one. If I don't try any of the really expensive ones, I'll never know what I'm missing," I reasoned.

Over the course of a few weeks, I lost a total of thirty pounds training. I also recruited a fellow Rotarian and the School Superintendent. We trained together and it quickly became obvious that it wasn't a bike ride - instead, it was a mission. I completed the 100-mile journey that day, crying most of the way.

Each rider rides for a particular missing child. As I opened my packet, with my jersey and pin, I noticed the child I was riding for was Shawn Googin. I saw that face, and was shocked that I remembered meeting Shawn one day when I had worked in Cazenovia at the Eidos Program, some twenty years ago. It was quite a coincidence, I thought. Halfway through the Ride, at one of the school stops, I was getting water and came across a volunteer in a red shirt. She looked at me, stopped, and looked up. She said, "You're riding for my son, Shawn." I looked with a blank stare, and my eyes pooled with tears. I couldn't keep it in, and hugged her. I said, "I met Shawn, a long time ago in Cazenovia. He was a really nice kid," I said solemnly. As we were hugging, it felt right that we had met that day. I could have bumped into anyone. I could have had any pin. But I quickly realized it wasn't by chance; it was by design.

Not only did I finish the Ride that day, I started an effort at the Y to train all of our staff in child safety and prevention through NCMEC. I also served on the Board of Directors of the YMCAs of New York State and was asked to serve as the Chairman of the Child Safety Task Force. In my role on the committee, I was able to bring resources to the forty-five other YMCAs in the state and create a Child Safety Toolkit, something that would make our organizations safer for children.

Frank Williams was one of the founding fathers of the Ride back in 1993. He and a small group of others rode from Central New York to Washington DC to bring awareness to the country about the events surrounding the abduction of Sara Anne Wood. Bob Wood, Sara's father, led a team of volunteers on the mission to bring both awareness and an end to all missing children. Sara's cousin, Tracy, is an Oneida resident and an old friend. I hadn't seen her too often, but as the Ride neared in 2012, my second year as a rider, Tracy called me and asked if I would ride for Sara. She said she had something for me, and brought it up to the Y the morning of the opening ceremonies. It was a loosely wrapped Sara Anne Wood t-shirt, cloaked in a teal bow, one of the original shirts made to help find Sara. There was a card inside that said:

"Dear Hank- as I read your article pertaining to the Ride for Missing Children, the emotions on that fateful day in August 1993 came flooding back with a vengeance. I was newly married at the time and had just learned that we were expecting our son, Eric. Phone calls, posters, rallies...Sara was everywhere and nowhere all at the same time. She was beautiful, charismatic beyond belief, and just as bright as bright can be! To watch my family try to make sense of her disappearance was just plain awful, and as a nurse who was trained to heal, my feelings of helplessness were often overwhelming. As the years have gone by, I have never forgotten one minute of our family's ordeal, but I have learned how support and strong commitment have the power to help bring people together in amazing ways. Thank you from the bottom of my heart for taking on the Ride for Missing Children and doing it proud - there is a beautiful little angel up above who is smiling her beautiful smile and who will safely guide you along your way tomorrow. I have taken her photo shirt out and if you would like, take her along with you - I am certain she would love it. Love and God bless - Tracy."

That day, I woke up as sick as a dog. I was coughing, sneezing, and barely able to open my eyes. But I had a 100-mile, twelve-hour bike ride in front of me. With Sara's shirt in my back pouch, I got up to the podium at the Y to give the opening speech. I took out my card from Tracy and read it to myself silently, just before

I walked to the microphone. I looked up at 500 people in the Y gym, and there was Tracy, looking right at me from the right hand side of the gym. She was giving me an encouraging nod. I smiled, then my eyes started to pool again. No cold, flu, or broken limb would have prevented me from riding that day. All along the way, I felt a peaceful, encouraging presence with me. It was calming and moving at the same time. I have no doubt that Sara was with me, and God was on my bike with me.

God called.

"The LORD upholds all who fall
and lifts up all who are bowed down.
The eyes of all look to you,
and you give them their food at the proper time.
You open your hand
and satisfy the desires of every living thing.
The LORD is righteous in all his ways
and faithful in all he does" (Psalm 145.14)

CHAPTER 6

Weeks later, my dad called and asked if my three sisters and I would all come over to the house. This wasn't by any means a normal request. It would be an understatement if I said my curiosity was piqued. In fact, I was scared. I pulled into the driveway and was the first one there. My mom met me at the door crying and immediately threw her arms around me. I tried to prepare myself for what was to come, but at the same time try to remain strong in case I was going to be needed to serve as the one the girls would rely on. I always feel like that is my role.

My sisters Terri and Sandy were next to arrive, followed by my oldest sister Debbie. We sat quietly on the couch and chairs in the living room as my dad spoke. "I have cancer; it is in my throat, and it's not good." We all felt that familiar lump in our collective throats. My sister Terri began to cry, while Sandy and Debbie were somber and questioning. He went on, "I have to have a tumor removed, and it's an aggressive one. They're going to schedule the surgery right away." We asked a few questions and I tried to stay strong, holding back the tears.

For the first time, we were scared. Our father - the rock, the patriarch from the old guard, the one who never flinched at the site of a challenge - was visibly shaken. Mom was petrified. We all were looking for some way to try to believe that it wasn't true. People tend to think their loved ones are going to live forever. My dad had always said, "Everyone has to die of something, you know." We used to tease him that wouldn't happen for a long time; but this time, it was for real.

We left the house that day, the same family home we'd all grown up in, moved away from, and sporadically visited from time to time. This time, the house seemed cold and dark, instead of warm and welcoming. "I think we should all write him a letter, letting him know how much he means to us," my sister suggested. The thought of a letter like that made me feel like it would be a goodbye, like a tribute. "They don't do tributes to people when they're living," I thought. I suggested we write something positive, uplifting, strong. They agreed; we did. And we each gave him our letters. I hadn't seen my dad cry before, but when he got our letters and read them, he had to leave the room. I knew it was a moment of truth for him, my mom, and for us.

The surgery was scheduled and we all went to the hospital, nervous with negative thoughts. I think each of us had gone to church a few times, or we had gone to the St. Joseph's statue just outside the church on the North Side and prayed that my dad would pull through this. Though we had prayed before, it was nowhere close to the concentrated message we wanted to send to the Lord this time. In mine, I know more than a few times I asked God for forgiveness. I asked him to forgive my sins from the past, when I hadn't listened to my dad, or when we'd had a disagreement and I was angry, or when I was needed and just hadn't been around. I prayed that my dad would forgive me for failing to make a phone call, stop by, or just say, "I love you." I also prayed that my mom would stay strong and take care of him and us. If there is such a thing as "praying hard," I did it. And, I 'm sure my sisters and mom did too.

Just before Dad went in to his appointment, he held each of our hands, told us not to worry, and joked with the nurses and doctor. We felt he was using this as a way to appear strong. I had no idea it wasn't for show until I learned just how strong a man he is. If he had fear, it wasn't in his eyes, and it wasn't on his lips.

That day in the waiting room seemed to last for weeks. The doctor came out and told us Dad had come out of surgery and that they had gotten the tumor, but he would probably need radiation and chemotherapy treatments. We were relieved, but not jubilant. They wheeled Dad into the room, and he awoke. I'll never forget his words or the look on his face. "I'm alive! I'm alive!" he said, like a true fighter. I questioned quietly if I would be that strong, given the same circumstances. I reasoned that I probably wouldn't be. That's why he is the hero, my hero, and I am just the spectator. I prayed to God for a sliver of his strength. At that moment I remembered a Bible scripture that has always stuck with me: *Truly I tell you, if you have faith as small as a mustard seed, you can say to this mountain, 'Move from here to there,' and it will move. Nothing will be impossible for you"* *(Matthew 17:20).* All I needed was a sliver of faith.

The thought crossed my mind briefly that all of that praying must have done some good, or that the doctors really knew what they were doing. I reasoned that medicine had made many advances and this time, there might be hope. But I also remembered the verse and hoped that I could just believe, and move that mountain for my family. God answered my prayer.

Treatments for radiation and chemo were scheduled with the oncologist's office in Rome. I worked in both Oneida and Rome on a daily basis, and offered to take Dad to his appointments. I would pick him up early in the morning, drive to the office and drop him off, then return at the end of the day to bring him home. Along the way there, we would talk about the Mets, cooking, or the Giants, fishing, gardening or the weather. We'd also talk about cancer, its impact, and the resources available. I'd stop by during the day and bring him a chocolate shake or something to ease the soreness on his throat. He was the life of the room, talking recipes and trading Italian cooking secrets with just about everyone there. When I left, the nurse would always say, "You've got a great dad, Mr. Leo." I already knew that.

There were dozens of times I wondered if I was going to lose him. I wondered if my next trip would be the last one. I said my prayers every morning and every night - always thanking God for Dad, my mom, and my sisters. I didn't ask that God give the doctors the knowledge and skill to make him better. Instead, I cut right to the chase. I asked God to give me Dad for many more years. One time in particular, I told God that if he did, I would change. I told God that I would never say no when asked to help. I would never say no when Dad asked me to spend time with him. I would never say no when he asked if I wanted to go somewhere with him. I told God I would take care of my family. I'd made bargains in the past, but this time I meant it.

We went fishing three times that fall. Over time, the chemo and radiation took its toll on him. He lost a lot of weight and was weak. During a regular check up, the doctors notified him that he had a new tumor in his liver. This one was aggressive as well. He continued treatments for a long time. Mom told me that they had started going to church again. That made me feel good. My faith and relationship with God was growing stronger.

Each day, I said the same prayers and I kept believing what I heard back from God. It wasn't in the form of a voice; instead it was a feeling. Dad called me on a Wednesday night and said, "Can you go fishing in the morning?" I replied, "Yup, I can go," not even checking my schedule. It didn't matter what I had on it that day at work. It was going to be postponed. A deal was a deal.

I woke up and it was a clear, cool morning. I drove to the house and Dad and I went down to the lake. We put the boat in the water, had coffee with some of the guys, and made our way out. I sat in the back, while he was up front. I snapped a photo of him reeling in the first fish of the day. The sun was just coming up over the horizon. It was like a moment when a weary sea captain is heading into the storm ahead of him, and he is protecting his crew from harm or injury. I felt like the crew and he was my captain. I couldn't understand why I was the one feeling led, while he was hurting so much and his life was at stake. His strength was staggering. I remembered the story of Peter in the boat with Jesus.

I came home and wrote down this poem:

The Fisherman
(In Honor of My Dad, Hank Leo Sr.)

5:45 AM, the sun glistens on the cold, calm waters of Oneida
Lake.
The boat is loaded and secured to the dock; a single rope
steadies the floating salvation.
Coffee brews in the marina, the morning news is shared.
As the Fisherman climbs aboard his mighty metal steed
a grin creases his weathered face. It is time. There is nowhere
else he would rather be.

Out to Buoy 107 maybe; Southeastern wind headed this way.
A selection is made from the rows of handcrafted lures.
"What color are we using today?" asks his son.
Blue, like the water this morning.
Tens of feet of line weave in and out of the waves as the motor
gently trolls.

Early tomorrow morning yet another treatment awaits.
The sun will glisten off hospital windows
as he sits for hours in a chair, waiting patiently.
Tens of feet of IV line will weave in and out of those sharing a
similar day.

Tubes, needles, drips. There are many places he would rather be.

He remembers that Jesus said, "Follow me and I will make you fishers of men."

His boat was small, his message simple.
Many a man has learned from the Fisherman.
Like the walleye, his "eyeshine" gives him sight
Seeing, not *in* the dark, but *through* it. He reminds his son:
> "Arise early and seize the day.
> Live not for the moment but for the stay.
> Enjoy your friends, the calm, and the peace.
> Let not your approach to a challenge cease.
> Give me a test, a life-threatening chore
> And the Fisherman will show you how to even the score.
> How do I get my limit? you ask.
> 'Denial,' is the answer. It's no easy task.
> I refuse to believe they will not bite
> Just as I refuse to believe my end is in sight.
> Like the fish who takes the hook and the bait
> The Fisherman alone decides his fate.
> The lesson to learn is to never give in.
> Keep casting your rod and your back to the wind."

6:15 AM, like a fly landing on a reed
The line wiggles slightly and bends. Only the Fisherman can feel it.
A jerk and a reel in.

If he dies here today, he is happy.

Though the walleye are few, there is nowhere else he would rather be.

7:12 AM, back to the marina they head, catch in hand.

Told too many times, "You don't have long..."

Too often warned, "The end is close..."

It is not close. Not even close.

He smiles at his son and whispers, "Not today."

The poem went through many revisions, because I wanted to get it just right. I also had never written a poem before. I pulled out the photo I took on the lake and brought both of them to Varano Studios in Rome and asked if Tom Varano could make it into something special, to be given to my dad for Father's Day. I was pretty proud of what I did, but didn't know how he would react to it. It was wrapped, and I handed it to Mom, to give to him. I didn't wait to see him open it, I just left, kissing my mom on the cheek. She didn't know what it was either.

I stopped by a couple of days later and Dad wasn't home, but Mom was waiting at the door. "We really liked what you did, Hank. Dad took it with him in his truck, to show the guys. He didn't say much, but I could tell he was very proud of you," she said. I received a call on my cell phone later that day from Dad.

"I wanted to let you know that you did a great job on the poem and picture Hank, and I'm proud of you. I love you."

That evening, my prayer was a little different. I looked in my NIV Bible for a thought.

God called.

"My son, do not forget my teaching,
but keep my commands in your heart,
for they will prolong your life many years
and bring you prosperity.
Let love and faithfulness never leave you;
bind them around your neck,
write them on the tablet of your heart.
Then you will win favor and a good name
in the sight of God and man.
Trust in the Lord with all your heart
and lean not on your own understanding;
in all your ways acknowledge Him
and he will make your paths straight" *(Proverbs 3:1).*

You don't just open up an 800-page book and flip to something like that, right? Coincidence? Fate? Luck? Chance? I don't think so.

After years of battling cancer, Dad was a wonder, a medical marvel. The doctors told him they had never seen anything like this. They told him no one had lived long enough for them to treat in this fashion. He was given several periods of time to die.

I was led to believe I should prepare for him to no longer be with us. I think, no I believe, that God had other plans. Faith is strong and powerful, more powerful than anything. It was not science or chance. There is no one who can convince me otherwise. I began to write. I began to write for the paper, in a notebook, on a napkin, in my head. And, write I did.

CHAPTER 7

In the winter of 2011, I had just finished writing an article for the *Oneida Daily Dispatch* about my experiences with religion. It was pretty much about my inadequacies, my ignorance, and my humility. Apparently, there were a lot of other people who must have felt the same way. I received several phone calls, emails, and even letters in the mail from people I didn't know who said they felt the same way. It was enlightening to me. All I could think about was how many lost souls there are out in the world, those who are searching for something – anything – happiness, understanding, contentment, and peace – just like I was so many years ago. I would go into the grocery store or the post office and someone would comment, "Thank you for writing what you did. It made me feel less alone." I was surprised, a little comforted, but mostly, reminded that I was one of thousands who felt the way I did. Lost sheep.

Pretty much, I shared that I don't know much. I don't understand how it all works between faith and results, but there were some lessons I've learned that others might like hearing. So I wrote them down, and they were public. I guess that's the part that people felt they could connect with- vulnerability. Everyone is vulnerable.

During the following week, I went to the Regional Market with Pauline and my sister. We had just had one of those typical winter mornings where we had gotten two or three inches of snow overnight. One day it's forty degrees and sunny and the next it's twenty and blowing like a little kid on his birthday cake. Welcome to Central New York. We were on our way home from the market, coming down a road just out of town, and I looked to my right and saw an elderly lady with a shovel propped on her walker, trying to push the snow.

She appeared to be in her eighties and could barely walk. She had on an old nightgown, in the cold of winter. She was barely moving and the shovel wasn't even touching the snow. The wheels of her walker were caught in the wet and heavy snow and it just didn't look like this was supposed to be happening. My sister commented, "I'm sure she has someone who takes care of her, right?" and my girlfriend commented, "Do you think?" We drove on, just like I had done a hundred times or more before in my life.

When we pulled in the driveway, I grabbed the shovel out of the garage and told Pauline, "I'll be right back, okay?" She said, "Take your time," understanding exactly where I was going. I went back to where I'd seen this woman but she wasn't there anymore. There was only one little path formed that barely exposed the asphalt, and it stopped well short of the road. I started at the road, throwing the wet snow over my shoulder and worked my way back toward the house. A screen door opened and I could see her looking at me through her thick, scratched glasses. She threw on a shawl and walked out. "I've been waiting for you," she said. "Excuse me, ma'am?" I responded with a dumbfounded look on my face. "I was just praying someone would come along and help me." I said, "Uh, I don't think..." I kept on shoveling.

I finished the whole driveway in just about an hour. She came out when I was finished and said, "Thank you so much." After about five long seconds of silence, I replied with appreciation, "No, ma'am, thank you." I hadn't given her anything that day. It was very clear that I was the recipient.

I wrote about that experience not long after the day it happened, again in the paper. Pastor Chris, whose weekly service is just a few miles down the road, read the article. He's a member of the Y and comes in several times a week. The day after the column ran, Pastor Chris knocked on my office door and asked if I'd be willing to speak at his church. Without giving it a thought, I agreed.

Let me remind you that I was brought up Catholic and had never attended a Methodist church. I don't think I'd ever even been in a Methodist church. I wasn't sure what to expect, nor was I confident in exactly what I was going to say. Mostly, I wasn't sure why anyone would want to hear what I had to say, especially in a church. And, to make matters worse, the truth is that all I had done was shovel a lady's driveway, something I've done a bunch of times in my life. But I had agreed because it felt right, and I really liked Pastor Chris. I also knew I had changed. I kind of felt like I *should* do this - if something good happened to me, I should pass it on to others. I still didn't think anyone would want to hear a word I had to say. I never do.

A friend of mine, Trish, gave me a few pointers as I prepared for my nervous public breakdown. "There are a lot of passages out there in the Scriptures that might help." She shared several and they were definitely moving, but I wanted to think of something that was unique to me. I went back to Barnes & Noble.

I was starting to become a regular in the "Christian Inspiration" section, sitting on the floor and reading whatever title appealed to me. The tall, Caramel Macchiato with extra whipped cream and a zig zag of real caramel helped, of course. On the bottom right hand side, there sat *The Promise*, by Robert J. Morgan. I took out a pen from my pocket and began making notes, kind of an outline for what I wanted to say in a strange church, where I've never attended mass, in a church other than Catholic, where I was going to be delivering a message to others, whom I didn't know, while hoping like crazy people wouldn't throw things at me or boo me. I prayed, right there in Barnes & Noble, for a good, strong cold to come upon me. A sniffle, a sneeze, anything. No luck. God wasn't going to let me off the hook.

I saw Pastor Chris on Monday before I was supposed to deliver my personal journey at his church on Sunday. He said, "Hank, you'll do fine. Remember, I'm not going to be there. My wife and I are going to see our son in North Carolina." I nearly vomited on the YMCA front desk. "Oh, okay, did I know that?" I thought. I'm sure he had said it before, but I was probably worrying too much by the request to hear it. I was alone again, but this time I had someone on my side, to keep me calm and focused.

Here are my actual notes in preparation for my day in church:

Dad...diagnosed with cancer; told us in living room (try not to cry)
Read multiple versions of the Bible (try not to sound ignorant)
Didn't know how to pray
Changed the words to make sense to me
Things started happening (try not to stutter)
Relationships and friendships improved
How do I learn to love another person? (Think of Mom)

Bible verse: He wants us to love others as we love him. It's not too late. This includes the sick, poor, enemies, everyone.

Help others. (Think of lady in her driveway)

Love them like He loves me.

Do something good for someone every time I think of myself. (Remember to say thank you)

Sunday morning came and, healthy as a horse, I delivered my "sermon." After I finished, several people came up and shared their appreciation. Trish happened to be in the audience that day and told me I'd done fine. Of all of the hugs and thank you's, the best comment was, "You did a great job," which was the most I was hoping for. Although I know it was an older gentleman just being nice, I felt for a moment that maybe God felt that way too. I have to admit that it was His approval I was trying to gain. It wasn't until I went home that day that I realized I had His approval before I was even born. From that day on, I have always been treated like family at Christ Methodist Church. God is alive there, and the people welcomed me with open arms. I also started revisiting my old church, and going to mass much more often.

God called.

May the God of endurance and encouragement grant you to live in such harmony with one another, in accord with Christ Jesus, that together you may with one voice glorify the God and Father of our Lord Jesus Christ. Therefore welcome one another as Christ has welcomed you, for the glory of God (Romans 15:5-7).

CHAPTER 8

Everyone has favorite things in life. We all do. I'm just not sure church experiences had ever fallen into this category. I've never heard anyone say, "You know, my favorite sermon was such and such." I mean there are people I've spoken to who have come back from church and I've asked what "the message" was, but they usually have a hard time remembering. I know I've done the same thing. It was the *going* that mattered, not what the priest or pastor said, which scripture was read, or what the meaning was. For most people, it was "I saw so and so in church. Wow, he doesn't look too good." Or, "I sat with John today. He seems to be doing okay; the kids are good." Nothing of substance.

I do have a favorite service though. And, I'll never forget it. I was in New Orleans for one of my frequent trips and decided to go to church on a Sunday morning at St. Augustine Church in the Lower Ninth Ward. It was not too long after Katrina and I decided I wanted, no, I needed, to go. Normally on vacation, I wouldn't even think of going to church, but things had changed. I sat in the back. I wasn't sure if it was a Catholic church, Methodist, or Baptist, but I set out to walk there and go in. Just past Louis Armstrong Park, nestled in the hub of the melting pot of American culture, jazz funerals and second line parades, just around the corner from the Back Street Cultural Museum, sits this wonderful national treasure.

The pastor was a Japanese man, who was soft spoken, humble and funny. There was a lot of singing, which I enjoyed, and a typical Catholic mass. I was surrounded by people of all cultures, from tourists to locals, black, white, Hispanic, Asian, you name it - all of the things that make my "second city" great. I felt right at home. At the end of the service, the pastor personally delivered an a cappella version of the great Louis Armstrong classic *What A Wonderful World* that made the little hairs on the back of my neck stand up. At the end, he commented softly, "Happy birthday, Satchmo."

I was so pleased to hear a pastor, in a big church, with hundreds of people praying aloud, to utter that. Not just because I am Armstrong's number one fan, but because of his next line: "Louis saw the world as a beautiful place, his playground, where people of all colors, creeds, and makeups come together for a common cause - to celebrate life." I thought that maybe that was what Jesus was trying to tell us, and do for us.

> *I see trees of green and clouds of white*
> *The bright blessed days and the dark sacred night*
> *And I think to myself, what a wonderful world.*

When it was time to offer peace to the person sitting next to us, I looked over at an elderly woman, maybe in her late eighties, who said to me, "Peace be with you, dawlin'. Thank you for sittin' with me." It was that simple. It was that nice. It made me feel good and special. I felt warm and comfortable in a place that I had never been and didn't know anyone. I said to myself, "If this is what church is supposed to be like, then I want more of it." It was the start of something new for me. It had nothing to do with color, or economic level, or status, or who was there, who wasn't there, or why they were there. I just felt at home, happy, and like I belonged. It was also because I had paid attention to the message. So I guess Louis Armstrong wasn't just a jazz singer that day. And I wasn't just a guy going to church on a Sunday. God called.

"Sing to the Lord a new song,
for he has done marvelous things;
His right hand and his holy arm
have worked salvation for him.
The Lord has made his salvation known
and revealed his righteousness to the nations.
He has remembered his love
and his faithfulness to the house of Israel;
All the ends of the earth have seen
the salvation of our God.
Shout for joy to the Lord, all the earth,
burst into jubilant song with music,
make music to the Lord with the harp,
with the harp and the sound of singing
with trumpets and the blast of the ram's horn-
shout for joy before the Lord, the King"(Psalm 98).

CHAPTER 9

Those who have pets might understand. A single guy and his dog are more than master and servant; they are best friends, confidants, compadres, walking buddies, talking buddies, counselors, and partners for life. Moms understand that dogs sometimes can sense things no human ever could. My dog, Louie Armstrong (go figure), a purebred Siberian Husky with all kinds of personality, is a big part of my life. I picked him up as a little puppy and we became best friends very quickly. He talks, howls, and sometimes speaks English. I swear I've heard him say "I love you" on more than one occasion.

At nearly ten years old, and a little overweight, Louie is aging and it's hard for me to see him at this stage. I struggle mightily trying to picture the day when he's no longer with me. And if you go by average lifespan, I don't have too many more years with him. It's a reality I just don't want to face. I mean, he's been with me through bad times, good times, and always stuck right by me- never wavering. How many friends can you say do that? Maybe one or two. Well, dog-lovers know what I mean.

Early one summer day, I came home from work and Louie was lying by the side of the house, as he always does. He didn't get up this time and come toward the car. I thought he just must have been hot. Huskies don't really like the heat, with the big fur coat and all. "Come here, boy," I said as I patted my thigh. He didn't move. I pulled on his leash, and he didn't budge. That hurtful lump in my throat began to reappear. Just then, he struggled to get up, then limped toward the stairs to the house and yelped loudly. I looked him over but it was clear he wasn't having any part of the stairs. I went in and called the vet, but it was a Saturday and the doctors were only on-call. The vet told me I'd better bring him in.

Louie's a big guy, around eighty-five pounds. For the first time in his life, I had to try to pick him up to get him in my car. He was crying and yelping even louder. As he usually can jump the length of a car with no problem, this time I was worried. My heart started to sink. I arrived at the vet and the doctor checked him out and told me that Louie definitely had done something to his back. It was hurting him. He mentioned that it appeared he had a disk problem. He said, "Why don't we go sit down in the office, Mr. Leo." I started to get uncomfortable in my chair, and my eyes teared. "Louie's an older dog. This problem is a serious one. I can give you a couple of options, but neither one of them is very promising, and they are both expensive. I can arrange for an appointment at a local university for you to have an MRI, as we don't do them here locally; or you could..." and there was a pause.

My eyebrows rose and my bottom lip began to quiver. "Or...?" I responded. "Well, as I said, he's an older dog and I don't know if you want to invest that kind of money to find out something that I think I already know. He most likely needs surgery. I can't be one hundred per cent certain until we see an MRI, but I'm thinking he has a disk issue, and it won't just go away." I knew I was going to face a tough choice. "How much are we talking about, Doc?" I asked. "Well over five thousand dollars," he responded quietly and with care in his voice. "Why don't you take him home and think about it. Here's the University's number. You can decide in the morning."

I cried all the way home and thought about Louie as a puppy. I thought about the rides we took on my bike and him running along with me. I thought about the walks we took together and how I used to talk to him like he was a counselor. I thought about losing him and wondered if I'd be able to handle it. I thought about my dad. "He's just a dog," I tried to reason. My feelings won the argument and I broke down crying again as I pulled into the driveway. I carried him, big bundle of fur and all, right up the stairs to the porch and into the living room. I sat on the floor next to him, and he put his head on my lap, which he has never done before.

"God, please take care of Louie. He's my friend. I love him as much as I love any other. He means the world to me. I know there are people suffering, and my needs don't seem as important in the grand scheme of things as all of the other problems in the world, but if you could save him, I'll be a better man. I promise." His chin lay to rest on my lap as tears flowed down my cheeks. I didn't bother getting up to wipe them off. I just sat there, for hours, praying.

The following day, I woke up, right in the spot where I was sitting. The floor was warm, and the sunshine was pouring through the curtains. Louie was not next to me. I began to wonder. "Dogs sometimes go off alone to die; where is he?" I looked all over the house, then walked upstairs. Louie was lying on my bed. "Are you okay, boy?" I asked with a trembling voice. Louie bounded off the bed and flew down the stairs, nudging his leash with his nose. He was running laps around the coffee table in the living room and jumping like a twelve-year-old kid on a trampoline.

Now, you can reason that the doctor misdiagnosed him. You can also possibly believe that he just "tweaked" something. You can maybe even assume he was just playing around. God doesn't heal dogs, does He? I don't think any of those things. I know what I know. I understand very clearly what happened. It wasn't all of those scientific or medical explanations and there isn't a scholar on the planet that can make me believe otherwise.

I am sure Louie will be with me in heaven. He and I will take walks every day. I'll run with him in the field and we'll fall on the ground, laughing and playing. The field will have no end. I won't get tired. And neither will my love. I thought to myself that God has no boundaries, and all you have to do is believe and ask.

After that day, I kept my promise. I decided to be a better man. I decided to not only be better to others; I wanted to *be* more to others. I reasoned in my heart that God's miracle of helping Louie, my Dad, and all of the other miracles was a chance for me to start something new, and to give something a try. I actually thought, and still believe, that God can appear in anyone, even a pet. Why not treat people as if Jesus himself was that person and testing you to see just how you might talk to Him, interact with Him and respond to Him? I remembered from church school that God could be anywhere at any time. He could be everywhere at the same time. He could appear as my neighbor, the stranger walking by, the little girl on the playground, the convenience store cashier, or in the face of an eighty-pound Siberian Husky.

I can tell you that when I started thinking that everyone I might meet, say hi to, wave to, or get to know could possibly be the

Lord Himself - things started to change. Saying hello to someone took on a whole new meaning. Whereas before, I might have been in too much of a hurry to pay attention to someone, I now stop and look them in the eye and let them know I am listening to them. Whereas before, I might have walked by someone who was poorly dressed, dirty, or sick, I now stop and ask if they need help. I can also look at someone and know instantly if they need help, are sad, cold, scared, or lonely. I've hugged people just after looking at them, because I've known.

God called.

"The wolf will live with the lamb,
the leopard will lie down with the goat,
the calf and the lion and the yearling together;
and a little child will lead them.
The cow will feed with the bear,
their young will lie down together,
and the lion will eat straw like the ox.
The infant will play near the hole of the cobra,
and the young child put his hand into the viper's nest.
They will neither harm nor destroy
on all my holy mountain,
for the earth will be full of the knowledge of the Lord
as the waters cover the sea" (Isaiah 11).

CHAPTER 10

It might seem righteous or weird to some. To me, I couldn't be more happy with my new "tool." Relationships improved. My faith became stronger. My interaction with my family grew closer. It didn't seem too out of whack to understand that if I asked myself, "What would Jesus do?", I'd be a better person, a better friend, a better caregiver, and a better man. I still make mistakes and I still get frustrated and angry. I am impatient and selfish at times, too. It just doesn't happen nearly as often as it used to and I consciously remind myself to fall back into line with my beliefs. When I do, things get straightened out in a hurry.

What used to be a life of selfish-focus has turned into a life of giving, helping, and being alive. Most people who experience some type of a revelation or "finding Jesus" do so with a near-death experience, a jail sentence, drug overdose, or a religious moment. They *see the light.* Mine took place in my living room, on the floor, with my dog on my lap. I didn't hear a voice and I didn't see a light. I was a "see it to believe it" guy for a long time. But I've come to understand that there are just too many "coincidences" for them to be coincidences. There are too many strokes of luck to call them luck. There are too many times when I said, "Wow, I can't believe that happened" for them to be "wow" things. Ironically, the only logical explanation I have is that God

89

is alive, with me, and I understand exactly what He wants me to do. It took me a long time to realize and believe it, but now that I do, I don't think there's anything I can't do.

God called.

"My son, if you accept my words
and store up my commands within you,
turning your ear to wisdom
and applying your heart to understanding,
and if you call out for insight
and cry aloud for understanding,
and if you look for it as for silver
and search for it as for hidden treasure
then you will understand the fear of the Lord
and find the knowledge of God.
For the Lord gives wisdom,
and from his mouth come knowledge and understanding.
He holds victory in store for the upright,
he is a shield to those whose walk is blameless,
for he guards the course of the just
and protects the way of his faithful ones" (Proverbs 2).

CHAPTER 11

Through my recent experiences, and my providing the "message" at Christ Methodist Church in Sherrill, NY, I made the effort to start going to church again. The first time, after my speaking engagement, I walked into the 10:30AM Sunday service. I wasn't sure where to sit or how I would be received. I really wasn't sure if I had done a good job or not the last time I was there. But I can say I was honest, it came from the heart, and I meant every word I had said. A beautiful, elderly lady motioned for me by patting the seat in the pew, just about halfway up in the middle. I joined her.

Winnie said to me, "I've been holding your seat for you," playfully. I responded, "Thank you for keeping it warm." She commented, "It's nice to see you, Hank. Glad to have you with us." I smiled and said, "It's nice to be back." I looked around the small church and saw many of the faces I had seen just a few weeks earlier. There were several waves, smiles, and warm signs of approval. I felt at home and among friends. Pastor Chris was there too, and smiled at me. I didn't recall ever feeling this welcomed before in any of my previous experiences. That's not to say it wasn't my fault, either. I could have reached out; I could have been more friendly then. I could have started conversations. I had just sat in the back and tried to keep quiet. This time though, I just felt, well, good.

Pastor Chris delivered the message that day about a news story that had just taken place heading into the Christmas season, where a volunteer from the Salvation Army was asked to stifle his trumpet playing, as he rang the bell outside of a store. His reflection was that this gentleman did not let a little order like that stifle his spirit, and he packed up and played elsewhere. As I sat there and listened, I looked around at the faces of others in church. They were nodding with approval and agreement that no one should dampen the spirit of anyone trying to do good, especially at Christmas time. And no one should put a damper on the Holy Spirit. I thought that the guy should have just played louder.

I also thought that maybe this happened to Jesus during His teachings and people probably kicked him out of places where he was preaching, in order to quiet Him down. I'm pretty sure Jesus did the same as this guy- he packed up and moved down the road. The rule didn't stop the mission; it only made more people pay attention to its necessity. I came to really like and enjoy Pastor Chris as a leader of his church, and I liked hearing his words.

I had a lot of questions for him and thought maybe he would be willing to help me along my journey. He was a member of the Y and usually came in during lunchtime. I had thought it might be a good time to meet, talk about life and God, and invite others to join us. So did he. Today, we are meeting weekly, and new people are joining our little group to share our thoughts, feelings, and to ask questions. It's really more about learning than it is following a particular denomination of religion. It's been very important for me to be there, to offer the Y as a place where people can feel comfortable in being healthy- spirit, mind, and body. In fact, I believe that the soul is equally important in everyone's health. I love my Wednesdays at eleven AM.

I had seen Pastor Chris dozens of times leading up to our meeting and never once thought that this beautiful and insightful gathering would come to my future. But I think Someone had other plans for me. I consider those in our group my brothers and sisters. I consider our lessons a way of communicating with the Holy Spirit. Where once, a long time ago, I may have hidden my beliefs or not shared my gifts, I now understand how important they are to others. I am humbled by the transparency, the openness, and the courage. There is no better path.

I also decided to start having breakfast every Friday with my good friend, Pastor Randy. We eat, pray, and talk about God, and I ask a lot of questions. We explore a lot of answers. We've hugged, cried, and laughed.

I've also returned to church, where I started as a little boy. The homilies have much more meaning to me now. The stained – glass windows are pictures I can understand. The ceremonies have meaning and communicate structure. The older ladies praying quietly mark hope for me and for others.

God called.

"Therefore, since we have been justified by faith, we have peace with God through our Lord Jesus Christ. Through Him we have also obtained access by faith into this grace in which we stand, and we rejoice in hope of the glory of God. More than that, we rejoice in our sufferings, knowing that suffering produces endurance, and endurance produces character, and character produces hope, and hope does not put us to shame, because God's love has been poured into our hearts through the Holy Spirit who has been given to us...." (Romans 5:1-11).

CHAPTER 12

The path I have taken to find my way was definitely the more difficult one. I often look at those kids I grew up with that are adults now, those who seem to have known their path right from the start. I used to marvel at them for the consistency of going to church, and "being religious." I never felt I really measured up, because I was always searching, always confused if I was doing the right thing. It wasn't until I started going to church again, being a part of the service, and really listening, that I came to feel at home. I also found that church is not in a building. Church can be wherever you are – on a street corner, at a convenience store, on a board of directors, talking to a friend, or a trip to the zoo. That seems to be my theme in life, at times- the road less traveled. I seem to always have taken the long way around to come to a conclusion I assume everyone else has already come to. But after meeting new people, talking with them, sharing my faith, and hearing theirs, I learned that I'm not so different after all. I guess I hadn't felt worthy before.

I recently came across Scripture that reinforced what I was starting to feel. The Lord spoke of a choice man has to make in Matthew 7:13-14, *"Enter in by the narrow gate; for wide is the gate and broad is the way that leads to destruction, and there are many who go in by it. Because narrow is the gate and difficult is the way which leads to life, and there are few that find it"* (NKJV).

What that means to me is that my path might not be all that bad. There are plenty of people who "go to church," regularly. But that doesn't necessarily mean they are there to listen, to learn, and be a part of a purpose. In talking to people, some of them just "go." It's the thing they do on Sundays and some do because they want their kids to grow up in the church and learn the importance of attending mass. Then there are those who love the fellowship, the public confirmation of believing, and those who collectively want to pray for loved ones. Those are the people I want to be around. They bring sunshine.

When I started attending some additional services, participating in my Bible study classes, asking questions, and gaining perspective, I began to feel for the first time that it was important for me to be there, necessary for me to listen and to be intuitively and instinctually committed to something. The unique thing that happened was the movement of my feelings and beliefs from routine to meaningful. And it never felt so special. The people I have met, the feelings and beliefs we have shared, the strength of identifying as a group – all has contributed a powerful combination of harmony and peace. I realize that my little narrow gate was a difficult one. It took me a long time to get where I am. I know that I still have a long way to go, but this path leads to life, not destruction.

God called

"And let us consider how to stir up one another to love and good works, not neglecting to meet together, as is the habit of some, but encouraging one another, and all the more as you see the Day drawing near" (Hebrews 10: 24-25).

CHAPTER 13

I didn't really understand completely what it meant if someone asked you to be their Power of Attorney. I guessed it just meant that you were able to sign things for someone who was unable to do so in the case of an emergency. It didn't really register with me until my friend John was called into active duty in Iraq, when the war first started and he asked me to be that guy. John was in the National Guard, and at the time, we weren't supposed to go into any war, and the likelihood of the Guard getting called into duty was pretty remote. Just after 9/11, when President Bush ordered our troops to Iraq, John was called up.

John and I have been friends since we were four or five years old. We went through school together, community college, even getting our degrees together at SUNY Cortland. We worked together after college and remain best friends even today. Just before he was deployed, we had a brief conversation over the phone. "Hank, I'd like you to be my Power of Attorney," he said with a little hint of anxiety. "Sure, buddy, whatever you need," I responded, not fully knowing or understanding what it meant. I was just happy to help him. "What do I have to do, John?" I asked. "I'll send you some paperwork, okay?" he said.

John had just gone through a divorce, and he was leaving behind his two sons. This proved very difficult for him, and I am sure he never imagined getting "called up." But this time, it was real. We were going into a war no one really wanted or had expected. The country was split in believing whether or not we were supposed to go to the country where weapons of mass destruction were supposed to be, but never found. It was dangerous, volatile, and unsettling for all of us, but for John, even more so.

Though he didn't say too much about the war or about his role, I knew that he was nervous-probably more because of leaving his boys than any direct combat he might have to face. There was always that uncertainty, though. What I didn't feel when he asked me that difficult question, I certainly began to feel on the day he left.

"My best friend is asking me to take responsibilities for his legal affairs in the chance he is killed in a war," I began to surmise. *"He needs someone to take care of his family, his sons, his home, his finances and assets, if he doesn't return, and he has entrusted me,"* entered my mind next. I wanted to call him and tell him how much I now understood the request, what it must have meant for him to ask me, and that I understood the seriousness of what he was going through, but it was too late. He had gone.

I was able to stay in touch and send him small packages, letting him know we missed him and everyone was thinking of him. I tried to keep it light and fun, and would send him mix tapes of comedy routines to keep his spirits up. I didn't want him to worry as I knew he had enough to worry about, but I am sure in his mind he was heading into a bee's nest, filled with the possibility of thousands of attacks, in a country that didn't want us there. He didn't want to be there, either. What this showed was his loyalty to his country, his commitment, his courage and his heart.

John had never been perceived as a leader growing up. He would usually follow in whatever direction the crowd was going. But the military changed all that. Being summoned to a war made him a hero, one that others would have to stand up and take notice of. I am not sure many people I know could have done what John did. Courage is sometimes very difficult to define. There are plenty of quotes out there to support acts of valor. I said many prayers for John while he was away. I prayed that he would return home to see his boys grow up. I prayed that he would lead others with his usual diplomacy and kindness. I prayed that he would make it home safely. And I prayed that if he didn't, I would be able to do justice in taking care of everything he needed me to.

Being courageous means having great character. It means putting aside fear to get a job done. What John did, without even knowing it, was provide me with the courage I needed to take on his burdens and responsibilities, to carry his cross if he needed me to. He gave me the strength needed to carry out his wishes for his family. I knew then that God would never abandon me if I needed Him, when John needed me.

God called.

"Be strong and courageous, and do the work. Do not be afraid or discouraged, for the LORD God, my God, is with you. He will not fail you or forsake you until all the work for the service of the temple of the LORD is finished" (*1 Chronicles 28:20*).

CHAPTER 14

During my teen years and even into college, I always wanted to work with kids. It was my favorite thing to do. I always dreamed of some day opening up my own youth center or being the executive director of the Special Olympics. In fact, I had a whole plan to become the head of the United Way. A lot of my friends in college would ask me why I wouldn't rather make a lot of money as a stockbroker or a banker and then donate money to a cause. I always wanted to give my time. I knew that was more valuable. In school back then, there was a resource room – the room where the kids with special needs would go to get their classes. At the time, it was pretty common to tease kids with disabilities. The "R" word was another word for stupid.

To be honest though, I used to stop in the resource room on my study hall periods. I found it a lot more fun than studying anyway, and I really liked the kids in there. Many of my friends were like that, too. Kids can be cruel sometimes, but a lot of us felt pretty good sticking up for them when they were getting teased. It would be a trait that I would carry with me for the rest of my life.

I worked as a little league coach, a big brother, park program director, mentor, you name it. I always stood up for the weak ones and tried to be a source of strength. One summer, I worked for a national summer sports program at a local college with my friend Pat. I was a baseball coach. I had played baseball in high school and a little bit in college, and that summer was one of my best, and it changed my life. I was assigned to a young, maybe eight year old, blond-haired kid, with bright blue eyes. His name was Chris. One of the directors just asked me if I would look out for him that summer and told me that Chris doesn't talk. He said he didn't know why, but he hadn't spoken in a long time. I didn't ask any questions, and didn't care, either.

Every day, I would get out the baseball equipment and bring it out to the diamond and take kids through batting, pitching, and fielding drills. I'd talk about Hank Aaron and how the Mets might win a World Series that summer. The kids all thought it was great because their home life didn't give them too many chances to participate in sports, let alone at a college. I would sit with Chris after the group was gone, and talk to him underneath a big old elm tree. He would fiddle with his sneaker laces and I would show him how to hold a bat. He would grip it tightly and make a half-hearted effort to swing it. Sometimes I would toss up a baseball and let him try to hit it. "Great try, buddy!" I would encourage as my voice rose in anticipation of a response. Just a smile came, but that was enough for me.

Weeks passed and the summer was an awesome one. It reinforced what I wanted to do for a career, and it made me happy every day. On the last day of the program, I was picking up the balls, bats, gloves, and catcher's equipment and putting them away in the big canvas bag, as it lay on the ground near home plate. One of the kids yelled to me that everyone was looking for me in the gym. I had forgotten there was some closing ceremony and everyone was supposed to be in there for it. I hurried along and walked in the back door.

When I opened the door, first, a clap, then another, then another, with every step I took. I looked around in embarrassment to both sides of the gym, as I thought I was walking into a ceremony, the last one, and interrupting something important. The clap turned into an all-out applause, with "Woo Hoo!" and "Yeah!" echoing through the walls. It took me several minutes to realize the applause was for me.

I went up to the stage, in shock, looking around at almost about 100 kids cheering. The director said, "Hank, we'd like to present you with the Coach of the Summer Award," as he smiled. I looked down and there was Chris. With a medal in his hand, he motioned for me to bend down. Putting the lanyard around my neck, he whispered in my ear, "Thank you." Speechless, I cried, then walked back down the aisle. I sat in the back row, blown away by what had just happened.

One of the other directors came up to me and said, "Hank, that's quite a compliment. Chris's mom used to bring men over to her apartment a few years ago. She didn't want the gentlemen to know that she had a child, so she put him in the closet and told him that if he made any noise, she would hurt him. He hasn't spoken since. Until now."

It was then I realized the power of the words *thank you.*

God called.

"His divine power has granted to us all things that pertain to life and godliness, through the knowledge of Him who called us to His own glory and excellence, by which He has granted to us His precious and very great promises, so that through them you may become partakers of the divine nature, having escaped from the corruption that is in the world because of sinful desire. For this very reason, make every effort to supplement your faith with virtue, and virtue with knowledge, and knowledge with self-control, and self-control with steadfastness, and steadfastness with godliness, and godliness with brotherly affection, and brotherly affection with love" (2Peter 1:3-8).

CHAPTER 15

I have always been what I would call "peripheral" in my relationships. Either I have been afraid to commit to them or I have led others to believe there was going to be more when I didn't have the capacity or the courage to give more. I never wanted to get too close to anyone or let anyone get too close to me because I was afraid the relationship *would* succeed, if that makes any sense. I was afraid that they would work, and then I would screw them up.

I've had thousands of friends, but they gave more to our friendship than I did. And I've had many intimate relationships that were the same way. I have felt terrible, disgusted with myself, guilty, and sad. I was like that with my family too -never letting them get close to me. At most functions, I sat quietly, not offering much, and wondering when the time was to leave. I was somber, ignoring the love that was around me. Inside, I was dying to be a "wear it on your sleeve, say what's on your mind, tell it like it is, and put it out there" kind of guy. But on the outside, I was stone-faced, cold, and withdrawn. I was afraid to risk, to take a chance, and to be who I am. The worst part was, I don't even know why.

My relationship, for most of my life, with God, was the same way. He was trying to provide for me, care for me, support me, help me, and surround me with love. I didn't give it back or pay attention. He was giving me all kinds of signs and I was looking the other way. He was shaking me and saying, "I'M RIGHT HERE!" and I didn't even listen.

It wasn't until I started reading the Bible, asking questions, and understanding it, that things came into focus. And it took me a long time. It was then when I figured out that it's okay to be loved and to give it and show it back; I began to change. I always felt that I needed to be in control and to calculate every risk, option, possibility that was out there in order to be happy. "Letting go" was never in my vocabulary. When I saw a bumper sticker once that said, "Let go; let God," I wasn't even sure what it meant until I went home and thought about it. And, letting go wasn't ever an option. The phrase meant that I can't be in control of everything and that there's no way I would make progress if I stayed locked in that cage. If I'd let God take care of me, I needed to trust that He would. It was one of the most enlightening days of my life, and it came from a bumper sticker.

I used to worry about the weather. I would worry about my car, my job, my hair, my health. I would worry about others and their burdens. I would worry about their health and happiness. Pretty much, all I did was worry. And it wasn't healthy. My weight was up and down. I would start and stop things. I was afraid to be who I wanted to be and I felt time was running away from me. Calendar pages seemed to flip by like I was thumbing through a magazine. I prayed to God to help me stop the worry. There was no lightning bolt or voice in my head. I just started reading the Psalms again. I read Psalm 55:22: *"Cast your burden on the LORD, and he shall sustain you: he shall never suffer the righteous to be moved."* I wondered if I would be able to do it. It seemed so risky, like giving all of your worries away and just exposing yourself to more worry. It didn't seem possible. I was nervous and scared, but decided to give it a try. When I finally did, there was a sense of relief, like letting go of a balloon or a paper airplane off a mountain. The interesting thing was that I knew I could fly and I believed that with a good tailwind and a safe co-pilot, it was going to be an adventurous, exhilarating, and exciting flight.

I reached out to my old friends and made a commitment to be a better friend and a better person. I even reached out to people I had hurt before and let them know I was sorry, and meant it. I opened up to my family and began showing them who I really am. In reality, I tried to be me. I started to pay attention to the signs around me, to the miracles that happen every day, and to the people I work with, work for, and who work for me. I tried to be a better supervisor, a better communicator, more compassionate to them. I didn't change who I was; I became who I am.

I paid attention to God. I purposely sought to surround myself with positive people who cared about others, weren't selfish, and put their needs behind the needs of their friends and families. I read book upon book of stories that inspire and stories of heroes, against-all-odds winners, and down-on-their-luck believers. I stopped watching horror films and replaced them with movies about hope.

I looked for people in need and researched the best ways to help them. And I began to write. The words just flowed. I had God's attention, and wanted to prove to Him that He hadn't invested in the wrong guy. Coming to the realization that he loved me even when I wasn't doing these things was even more important to me. He'd stood by me, trusted me, and knew who I was. I was the one who didn't. Now I believe that I have a lot of years to make up for the time I hadn't paid attention. I came to the conclusion that it's never too late to win the grace of God, to learn, to surround yourself with His spirit, and to be exactly what you were made to be - a child of His- a beautiful creation that lives to be a shining light for others when they are in the dark.

God called.

"So if there is any encouragement in Christ, any comfort from love, any participation in the Spirit, any affection and sympathy, complete my joy by being of the same mind, having the same love, being in full accord and of one mind. Do nothing from rivalry or conceit, but in humility count others more significant than yourselves. Let each of you look not only to his own interests, but also to the interests of others. Have this mind among yourselves, which is yours in Christ Jesus ..." *(Philippians 2: 1-30).*

CHAPTER 16

Have you ever felt like people were placed in your life for a reason? We all have those great friends that come through for us, when we need them most. It could be when we experience the loss of a loved one, as we are going through a divorce, managing teenagers, dealing with a difficult situation at home, school, work, or just plain old life. Every once in a while, someone just magically happens to appear, say the right thing, comforts you, makes you feel better, and just "gets" you. I've come to learn that maybe that's not by coincidence either.

Just like the angel appeared to help those who wondered if Jesus was returning after He died for us on the cross, I believe God places angels in our lives, at just the right moments, for just the right reasons. It's not by chance. It's not a coincidence and it isn't plain, old-fashioned luck. On the contrary, it's intentional, carefully thought out, strategic, and by design. At least, that's what I believe.

There have been so many times, when something bad just happened, that it seemed like life stopped and I wanted to get off, that someone would say or do just the right thing at the right moment. I remember one time when I was President of my local Rotary Club, I was giving the opening speech and welcoming everyone. The agenda hadn't changed in a Rotary meeting in a hundred years, and I was just reading off a sheet and following an agenda, when I completely forgot where I was and what I was doing. It seemed like maybe I was losing my mind. I just wanted to get away from the podium, pass by everyone, and walk out the door. But I made it through.

At the end of the meeting, a local pastor and Rotarian came up to me and whispered in my left ear, "You know, Hank, the first sign of stress is forgetfulness. We're saying prayers for your Dad at mass every Sunday. He's going to be okay." I wasn't sure how she knew what was going on with me. I knew I hadn't really talked about it with anyone. My response to her was, "I'm sorry." I don't know why I said that, or what I really meant by apologizing for forgetting something in a meeting, but she knew that something was bothering me, and she wanted me to know that I was in good hands. That was the day my dad started his chemotherapy and radiation treatments.

It was also the day that I prayed, non-stop, all day. I realized that toughness and strength have nothing to do with putting on a false face. I realized that it was okay to show pain, suffering, and a feeling of hopelessness. Reverend Betsy's comment to me made me human, at a time when I didn't want anyone to know I was. That helping hand, that vote of confidence, that one, small seemingly meaningless statement made me understand that there were things beyond my control and it was okay to let someone else bear the pain.

God called.

"It was revealed to them that they were serving not themselves but you, in the things that have now been announced to you through those who preached the good news to you by the Holy Spirit sent from heaven, things into which angels long to look" (Peter 1:12).

CHAPTER 17

As years pass and the Christmas season begins to come upon me, I have learned to appreciate the day itself as much more than a work holiday. For the past several years, the marketing companies for the big chain retailers start playing Christmas songs before Thanksgiving. It made me sick to think that the birth of Christ was some marketing ploy to get people thinking about "Black Friday" and "Cyber Monday" just to increase sales of products. What gets lost is the true meaning and spirit of the season.

I wasn't even sure what it was any more. I went to the mall just before Christmas only to find rows and rows of kids sitting in director-style chairs, lining the hallway leading up to a sneaker store. When I asked what everyone was doing, the 18-ish kid, with his head in an oversized baseball hat flipped backward said, "The new Jordans are coming out, man," referring to the latest Nike Airs being released to retail outlets. I responded with, "Merry Christmas." He put his headphones back on and slumped down into his chair, texting on his Smartphone.

Over the past year, I have had the wonderful opportunity to get together with a couple of great guys, on Wednesdays at the Y. We talk about things and get closer to what is really important in our spiritual development. It's kind of odd and cool at the same time that four guys get together just to talk about positive stuff. It's probably something I never would have done a few years ago. But it seemed good and right. This Christmas, our Pastor gave us a book to read and discuss. It is called "Christmas is Not Your Birthday," by Michael Slaughter, a pastor from Ohio. Its premise, of course, is that Christmas is not supposed to be about your presents, your gifts, commercialization, or material things. It is an "in-your-face" read about our own selfishness.

Doug, Kevin, and I all read the book, highlighted sections to talk about, and were ready to provide our input. At our meeting, we shared how we felt about Christmas. Kevin, a father of young children, struggles with trying to provide a traditional Christmas for his kids when he wants so badly to bring them the gift of Christ. He relayed to us that it is not an easy task. Doug has children who have grown, and wants desperately to find and become closer to Christ. It is easy to see that Doug is a little ahead of both of us. He knows what he wants and knows how to say it. I am somewhere in between. Our pastor does a great job of getting us to talk and share, alternating the speaking duties fairly throughout the conversations. He also gives us his personal take on Scripture based on his experiences. Our group has become a tight one and a productive one.

Leading up to Christmas, we had two or three sessions of discussion on the book. We all talked about wanting to become better at realizing the commercialization of Christmas and trying to avoid it. But as much as I would say I wanted to change my behavior, I couldn't help but find myself at Best Buy, Wal-Mart or some store in the mall, looking for gifts for Pauline and my family. I wanted to come up with things that mattered more or were not products, but I didn't want to give them nothing. This is why I still know I have a long way to go.

I had read where my church was having a live nativity scene and play, just before Christmas. I asked Pauline if she wanted to go. She said she would love to. The days leading up to the play were beginning to get cold, and it looked like a traditional central New York winter was headed our way. Just as all seemed somewhat normal, news broke of a young man who entered an elementary school in Connecticut and murdered a group of children and their teachers.

It struck us, and the country, like a knife in the heart. Locally, we all envisioned something like this happening in one of our schools, in our little town, and the shock wave of possibilities created fear and nervousness among all of our residents. In the midst of the discussions of stricter gun laws and anti-bullying campaigns, tougher awareness of mental problems facing young adults, school security, and the death of twenty-seven children and teachers sat Jesus Christ's birthday.

I felt like the world was falling apart. It seemed like there was no way Christ could be present in our world and allow something like this to happen- to innocent children. I remember asking Pastor Chris at our last session before Christmas how something like this can happen and he responded, "God gave us this world and we collectively said, 'Okay, thank you-we've got this from here, and don't need you anymore,' and took matters into our own hands." I nodded. I thought to myself that we had gotten so far away from allowing God in our lives, from taking it out of the schools, to the commercialization of His birth, even to murdering innocent people, that we're telling God we don't need Him anymore. That, however, clearly isn't working.

The live nativity scene and play was to be the next day. I asked Pauline if she still wanted to go and she said, "It's going to be freezing out, and maybe raining or snowing. Do you still want to go, Hank?" I responded, "I'm pretty sure it was cold in the manger too, and they still came." We both smiled and put our coats, gloves, and hats on. When we arrived outside of the church where the scene was set up, there were children scurrying to sit on top of the hay bales. A donkey was hitched to a small fence and what appeared to be three young adults in oversized Wise Men costumes were making their way to the spot where a baby doll was placed in the arms of Mary, with Joseph standing close by. The cold wind howled through the trees and it began to rain icicles. Pauline and I approached the crowd.

A friend I knew looked up at us as she sat on the bleachers in the front row, next to her daughter, huddled under a blanket. "Come sit with us," she said with a smile. We said, "No, that's okay Sarah; you sit there." She replied, "No, come sit with us. It's warm under the blanket and it's nice to see you and have you with us." We did sit with her, and watched the forty-minute play about the birth of Jesus, a story we had been told for decades. But it never had more meaning than it did this Christmas. I couldn't stop thinking of those kids and families in Connecticut and how they must feel about Christmas this year. I, on one hand, was sad and confused and on the other, so appreciative to be witnessing the birth of our Savior during such a rough time. I started to believe once again that His coming was to save us, and we needed to pay attention. I know I did. Sarah's hospitality during a cold, wintry night, just after a life-changing devastation led me to believe there was still hope. It was a gift, a true Christmas gift. It didn't cost anything and it meant the world to me. For just a moment, the murders and grief were engulfed in flames and the smoke rising to the heavens signaled a change. Chris was here.

God called.

"Through him we have also obtained access by faith into this grace in which we stand, and we rejoice in hope of the glory of God. More than that, we rejoice in our sufferings, knowing that suffering produces endurance, and endurance produces character, and character produces hope, and hope does not put us to shame, because God's love has been poured into our hearts through the Holy Spirit who has been given to us" (Romans 5: 2-5).

CHAPTER 18

"Three Teens Stabbed at East Fayette Street Apartment Complex" is what the headline read on January 6, 2013 in our local newspaper. The story was about three young people, all under the age of twenty, who were stabbed in a fight in their homes on a Sunday afternoon. This story is not unlike most stories that grace the covers of our news on a daily basis. It is so common and so routine to read about or see gruesome images of murder, rape, corruption, and death that I wonder what is happening to our world.

In 2013, young children are being fitted for protective, bulletproof vests. Teachers are being taught how to defend themselves with firearms, and there is talk of arming them as they come to our schools each morning. Babies are left for dead in dumpsters. And recently, a Canton, NY woman pled guilty to killing another woman found covered in burns and wailing in agony on the side of a rural road. What is the world coming to? What happened? How can this be happening?

I have such a strong, positive faith in people, and believe in the good in them. And yet, I hear these stories and don't know whether I can ever understand their roots or their reason. I get frustrated, sad, and defeated. It is then that I turn to the Bible.

On the same day I read those headlines, I stopped at Barnes and Noble to look for a new book. Heading through the front doors, I saw a man behind me and held the door for him. He said, "I've got this; you go ahead." I thanked him and walked in. Heading to the Christian Inspiration section, as I usually do, I sat on the floor and ran through pages of new books, trying to choose which one to buy.

I was searching, maybe even subconsciously, for something that would help me make sense of the world. I had recently become an author, writing my first book, called *Home When the Streetlights Come On*, which is a compilation of short, funny, and inspirational stories of my childhood and the innocence of those times. Being a new writer gave me a new perspective on reading other books, such as their way of making you think, feel, and believe in the words. Caught up in jotting down notes, I heard someone next to me clear his throat. I looked up and there was the guy who had held the door for me. He smiled and said, "I love this section too. It has a lot of answers for me." I responded, "I hope so; I'm looking for some, too." He walked away, and I chose a bright, orange-colored, thin book, with the title *Bees In Amber*. Randomly flipping to page 40, it said,

"He writes in characters too grand
For our short sight to understand;
We catch but broken strokes, and try

To fathom all the mystery

Of withered hopes, of death, of life,

The endless war, the useless strife,--

But there, with larger, clearer sight,

We shall see this—His way was right" [2]

Just because there is evil in the world, doesn't mean we need to be afraid. Power, love and self-control overcome fear, every time.

God called…

"For God gave us a spirit not of fear but of power and love and self-control." (2 Timothy 1:7)

---

[2] Oxenham, John. *Bees in Amber. A Little Book of Thoughtful Verse.* American Tract Society, 1913.

CHAPTER 19

I recall a time when I was sleeping and woke up from a dream where I was falling and could not yell. I didn't believe anyone could hear me. You know these dreams; we've all had them at one time or another. You are in danger, bound or tied, falling to your demise, when you wake up at the last moment, sweating profusely and thanking the pillow for reminding you that you are still alive. It was that kind of a dream on this night.

Since my love and relationship with God has grown, I don't fall anymore. And I believe that if I have those dreams again, that I will not be afraid. I know that if I do, or for some reason that I don't awake, I know I am falling into the arms of my Savior. There is no greater comfort than living without fear and lying in the arms of the One who created me, the One who would never let me slip, would never let me down.

At a recent service at my church, we were singing a hymn called *And Can It Be That I Should Gain?* As always, I was struggling with the music, but reading the lyrics a little more closely this time. At the end of the service, I didn't want to forget that hymn. I brought my bulletin home, circled the hymn and searched the lyrics on my computer.

The fourth verse reads:

"Long my imprisoned spirit lay,

Fast bound in sin and nature's night;

Thine eye diffused a quickening ray-

I woke, the dungeon flamed with light;

My chains fell off, my heart was free,

I rose, went forth, and followed Thee.

My chains fell off, my heart was free,

I rose, went forth, and followed Thee.

Still the small inward voice I hear,

That whispers all my sins forgiven;

Still the atoning blood is near,

That quenched the wrath of hostile Heaven.

I feel the life His wounds impart;

I feel the Savior in my heart.

I feel the life His wounds impart;

I feel the Savior in my heart" [3]

It is difficult for me to describe the freedom I have now. Life, for me, has changed and all of the things it proclaims. I pray now every night, and, I mean *every* night. All of my prayers are for others, for their health, their well-being and their safety. I sometimes pray for myself, but only for strength to help others. I really concentrate and think about what I am going to ask for

---

[3] Wesley, Charles. *And Can it be that I Should Gain?* Taken from
http://www.cyberhymnal.org/htm/a/c/acanitbe.htm

and why. There is only one prayer I ask for myself and I repeat it daily: *Dear Lord, please grant me my health, so that I can go on doing good for others and serving you.* I repeat it several times.

When I go to church now, I listen intently to the message. I find the scripture in my Bible and at night I re-read the verse and see what I think about it. I also look at and admire the beautiful architecture, sculptures, and stained-glass windows, feeling small and thankful for the time that was put into dedicating them to God. The closer I look at the "gargoyles," the more I see angels and saints looking down. I think of the nuns, their amazing dedication to the Lord and commitment to education. I am humbled by their ardor. I see the priest, pastor or reverend. I am thankful that they make the message new every time, for the little boy in the fifth row who might not be paying much attention, to the grown man who now stands solid in his faith, but wanting to learn more.

When I go to the alter for communion, it is no longer a dry, crisp wafer. It represents sacrifice and hope. And, I've come to understand that the wine truly is an endless cup. I am sharing supper with friends, those who believe in God, and those who want to receive Him.

It's common to write to someone who has lost a loved one, or going through a hard time, "You and your family are in my thoughts and prayers." When I type those words, or write out a card, I now sit quietly and pray for them. I always ask the person what their loved one's name is. I want it to be personal. I also don't want to simply type it, to make the person feel better. I want to think about it, feel it, and mean it. It feels to me as if I once was imprisoned in my own sorrow and lost in my soul, but that is gone now that I am sharing God's gift. What a difference it has made! I only hope I can be someone's light. My goal is to try to shine for them, and to help them shine too.

God called.

"You are the salt of the earth, but if salt has lost its taste, how shall its saltiness be restored? It is no longer good for anything except to be thrown out and trampled under people's feet. You are the light of the world. A city set on a hill cannot be hidden. Nor do people light a lamp and put it under a basket, but on a stand, and it gives light to all in the house. In the same way, let your light shine before others, so that they may see your good works and give glory to your Father who is in heaven" (Matthew 5:13-16).

CHAPTER 20

Over the years, I have come to learn several things about myself through my spiritual journey. I have always been a passionate guy about most everything important to me. It took me a long time to become a thinker, someone who studies, learns, and reasons. More than anything, for a great deal of my life, I just went through the motions. Great things would happen, bad things would happen. There would be huge successes and wonderful, inspiring challenges. It didn't come altogether for me very easily, as it does some.

Like a small child lost in the woods, I felt scared, alone, and wondering what direction I would go. It wasn't until I found Christ, through the help of dozens of people, books, experiences, and passion, that my world opened up to me. Not ironically, I found new friendships, meaningful ones, and looked at things in a new way. I started writing again, and it had improved.

There's a paragraph in Kahlil Gibran's *The Prophet* that I always remember. It says, "Your reason and your passion are the rudder and the sails of your seafaring soul. If either your sails or your rudder be broken, you can but toss and drift, or else be held at a standstill in mid-seas. For reason, ruling alone, is a force confining; and passion, unattended, is a flame that burns to its own destruction. Therefore let your soul exalt your reason to the height of passion, that it may sing; And let it direct your passion with reason, that your passion may live through its own daily resurrection, and like the phoenix rise above its own ashes." [4]

Amen to that. I'll do my best to keep trying, to improve. I know I can help others and know now that there are no limits. I can apply what I know and combine it with my love of God, and that of my family, friends, neighbors, and strangers, to be a better person.

I am constantly working on myself, always trying to improve. I have many faults and make as many mistakes as the next guy. I just have more awareness of the good that can come when I listen and participate in my life and in the lives of others, more than ever in the past. I attribute this to my new and growing relationship with God. I never want to go backwards. I am committed to growing. And, where I used to think I could control everything, I now know God is bigger.

Pretty much all of my life I have had one motivating factor. It rears its beautiful head every time. A common comment on my entire life has been, "You can't do that." Every time I hear that phrase, the only thing it does is motivate me to believing more in

[4] Gibran, Kahlil. *The Prophet.* New York: Knopf Doubleday Publishing Group, 1952.

"me" than they did. There's an old Peanuts comic strip where Lucy is yelling at Linus, telling him that his drawing is not art. She exclaims, "That's a terrible drawing! You have absolutely no talent!" He continues to draw, looking down at his paper, appearing to be disinterested in her mean comment. But if you are a guy like me, or anyone who's ever been in that situation, you are listening; you do care, and it does bother you. Lucy, out of frustration says, "No one ever listens to us critics…" and Linus continues to draw. I've decided to keep drawing too. My pictures have become much more beautiful now that I focus.

Inside, I know Linus is smiling, just like I have done a million times. I remember very clearly in high school being told by my guidance counselor that I should be an athlete. "Hank, you're a good athlete; maybe you should go to a community college and try out for the baseball team," she would say. I nodded an approval, knowing in my heart that I was meant for something more. I even wrote in a journal that I wanted to be a writer – and that was at the age of sixteen. Barely legal to drive, I knew what I wanted to do then. I did go to a community college and did play baseball, but quickly discovered that my true interest and love was to help people, write, and develop as many interests as I can. Tell me I can't do something and you just motivate me to do more. What does that have to do with God? What does that have to do with a spiritual journey?

I was hearing that, based on my grades, I was probably destined for mediocrity. I was hearing that I was marked to be what someone else had in mind for me. Her impression was based on a few meetings, a perception. I don't know. It wasn't her fault. In reality, I have her to thank for opening up my mind and my eyes. After a lot of years of trying to prove her wrong and convincing myself that I wasn't going to let someone else dictate my future or how I feel – trying to understand the concept of "let go, let God" was a tough one. It meant to me that I needed to let someone else again decide what was best for me. There was a difference this time, though. I believe God believes in me. He has never let me down. Every one of His words has come true. He has shown me compassion, honesty, humility, sacrifice, forgiveness, and most importantly, the art of standing naked and transparent.

I also know that people might say, "Since when did Hank become religious?" It doesn't really matter to me anymore when it happened. What is important is that it did, and I am still trying like crazy, making mistakes, and learning from each one. I am by no means an expert. I never feel like I am finished. But, I've learned some things that I can now share:

- It's never too late to start.
- It doesn't matter what anyone else thinks. You are your own soul's captain and your journey starts with believing.

- Pay attention to the little things. There are signs all around that God is with us. Don't ignore them.
- Be thankful for what you have and what you've lost
- Open up your heart and your mind. Great things will happen.
- Give more and take less
- Ask for forgiveness from those you have hurt, including God
- Love your family and your friends like there is no tomorrow; love God like there is a tomorrow

Lastly, you don't need to impress God. God doesn't want or need to be impressed. He's going to judge you simply on believing Him, how you treat others and He will love you listening to His word. The closer you get to Him, the better your life is going to be. He's got your back. He does listen. And, even though things may not make sense at first, they always do in His plan. And, He loves you enough to include you in it. Is there anything better than that?

God called.

"Do your best to present yourself to God as one approved, a worker who has no need to be ashamed, rightly handling the word of truth" (2 Timothy 2:15).

CHAPTER 21

After all this time, I'm still jotting notes, whether it's at Barnes
and Noble, a Rotary meeting, concert, or a "sermon" at a local
church. Sometimes the words just come to me, and I need to
borrow a pen or pencil, and a scrap paper. It's common to find
me hastily scribbling thoughts when something I hear or see
touches me in a certain way. Recently, while sitting quietly in
Sunday mass, I recognized the beloved hymn *Amazing Grace*. I
had heard it thousands of times, but this day, at St. Joseph's
Church, I wrote this on a napkin:

Amazing grace (Think about the love and mercy the Lord has for
me)

How sweet the sound (The sound of a baby breathing, the
heartbeat of a revived patient)

That saved a wretch like me (Why do I deserve it? Because He
loves me)

I once was lost, but now I'm found (I am grateful to those who
have helped show me the way. It feels good to be home)

Was blind but now I see (Blind to the ignorance, afraid to believe,
and scared to show it. Those have come to pass)

'Twas grace that taught my heart to fear and grace my fears relieved (Asking for forgiveness and receiving it cleansed my soul)

How precious did that grace appear, the hour I first believed (The light went on, I understood, now it is time to share with others)

Through many dangers, toils and snares…we have already come. (Life hasn't been easy and there are problems all around us) 'Twas grace that brought us safe thus far. And grace will lead us home (Trusting in God is the only way to find salvation and peace)

The Lord has promised good to me. His word my hope secures (It is all there in the Scriptures for me to read, understand, and believe)

He will my shield and portion be as long as life endures (I am no longer afraid. My faith is strong)

When we've been here ten thousand years, bright shining as the sun, we've no less days to sing God's praise then when we've first begun (Now that I am here, I am never turning back)

Amazing grace, how sweet the sound, that saved a wretch like me.
I once was lost but now I'm found. Was blind, but now I see (I hope
you will too)

God called.
God calls.
Amen.

EPILOGUE

I recently found an old scrapbook of mine that my mom gave to me for Christmas. As I thumbed through the plastic page holders that encapsulated my childhood memories, I noticed a typed letter on faded orange paper entitled "Summertime." Handwritten in the upper left hand corner, it says "Dear Henry," and it is signed, "Sister Carmelite." It reads:

"Summertime is almost here. For days and weeks you will not have any school (church school). But do not forget all the things you have heard in school. Remember that God wants boys and girls to think of Him and love him during the summertime too.

Here are some of the things you will do if you love God:

Say your morning and night prayers.

Go to Mass on Sundays and on August 15th, which is a Holy Day

Wear Blessed Mother's medal around your neck.

Keep God's name holy at work and play.

Obey your mother, father, and all who take care of you.

Be kind to others at home and at play.

Do not take things or keep things that belong to others.

Be pure in your thoughts, words and in everything you do.

Always tell the truth even if you know you will be punished for something.

Be sure to be modest in your dress.

I know you will be faithful children, and at the end of the summer you will be happy to tell God you have spent the summertime well. I have enjoyed teaching you during the past months and will miss every one of you. In the meantime, we look forward to meeting again in the fall. Be good boys and girls. May God bless and keep you close to him."

As I reflect on my spiritual journey and see the words on this forty-year-old page, I am reminded that the message has not changed much and this advice is as good today as it was then. It doesn't really matter which path you choose or how you get there- though I know I took the road less traveled. What really matters is that I came, through many trials and errors, to a realization that I needed to come to. It wasn't until I opened my eyes and paid attention to the signs around me that I understood God had called me repeatedly. I ignored the signs, wrote them off as luck, coincidence, or chance. The truth of the matter, for me at least, is that I'm a better person when I believe. And that is something no one can doubt, and no one can ever take away from me. The best part of the "gift" is that I feel like I'm supposed to pass it on to as many people who want it.

"Father of light, you have given us your Son to be our light. He has led us out of the darkness of sin into the light that is love.

Help us all to deepen our conversion and to be truly children of the light."

(Quote from "First Penance, St. Joseph's Church, March 23, 1974.)

POST SCRIPT

During the writing of "God Called," my Dad passed away. It was July 21st, 2013, one of the saddest days of my life. People asked shortly after if I was mad at God, if I had lost my faith, if I stopped believing. After moments of solitude, reflection, and a smile, I responded that God did exactly what I thought He would do. He answered my prayers. He called. He wrapped him in His arms, and took away his pain. He brought Mom and her four kids closer together. He made my faith stronger.

It was such a difficult time – I worried whether or not I would get through it. During the whole process, Pastors Randy, Chris, Jeff, and Father Mike were there with me – either in person, with words, or prayers. And, so was my incredible family and friends.

Knowing I write a weekly column for the paper, and my deadline was approaching shortly, this one was going to be THE one. I wrote it in one sitting, without any edits or changes. I didn't even re-read it after I wrote it. It just came from heart to hand, and it appeared in the Sunday edition of the Oneida Dispatch the week Dad went to heaven:

It's taken a couple of days now for me to finally write about losing my dad, Hank Leo Sr. At first, I wasn't sure I wanted to write anything, because I was so sad, and I didn't want to believe he was actually gone. Then, I didn't want to write just about my dad, as plenty of my friends and others have lost theirs too and I now share their pain. So this one is for all of the people who've lost their moms or dads. With over 2,000 people visiting us during calling hours, the funeral and at the cemetery for an amazing tribute to my hero, I wanted to thank everyone for the genuine care, concern and love that surrounded me and my family. Many people, while hugging me in line commented, "I'm looking forward to learning more about your dad in your column."

On the prayer card, my family decided on a photo of Dad I took when we were fishing over a year ago. I took it from the front of the boat, as he was casting a line out from the back. The sun had just come up that morning on Oneida Lake and you could see the soft, orange globe creeping up in front of him, leaving a majestic backdrop for what would become a famous picture of the person I admired the most. You see, I was fishing because of a conscious effort I made to spend more time with him, during the nearly daily treks to Rome for his chemotherapy treatments. I would pick him up at home, drive him to the oncology center, and stop there on my way back to Oneida after work to drive him home. Our time together was precious. We talked about all of the things that mattered. You know, gardening, cooking, fishing...all metaphors for what would become my life lessons. "Plant your seeds and make sure they take root. Water it, and make sure the stakes hold up the drooping tomato plants. Don't go by the recipe; go by taste. Get up early, work hard, get your limit, enjoy the catch, and share it with who you're with." Translation: Family first, always. Care for your family, neighbors and friends around you. Support one another. Trust your feelings. Celebrate life.

I've got it, Dad.

Not too long after one of the treatments, he asked me to go fishing with him. I had my cell phone in my pocket and wanted to preserve a memory of him. I focused while he was reeling in, and hit the button, but looked down and saw that it was on "video" by mistake. I quickly flipped the switch over to "camera" and snapped the picture. I went home that day and wrote a poem. It wasn't easy; I had never written one before. I wanted to weave his chemo treatments in and out of a fishing story, and give it to him for Father's Day. I worked on it for a long time, crying most of the time, until it came out just the way I wanted it. I dropped it off on the morning of Father's Day last year, and he was't home, so I left it with Mom. I didn't hear from him until the following day. "Hank, I got your picture and writing. You did a good job. I'm very proud of you, and I love you." My dad wasn't the kind of guy who shared his emotions very often, so that was a special message. My mom told me he was so proud of it, he took it with him in his truck and shared it with his friends at the Marina.

My dad was a fighter. He was such a strong, tough, solid guy, and a humble gentleman. It was hard for me to watch him battle for his life for over five years. I hate cancer. I hate that it takes lives from good people, and their families. I remember praying so hard, in church, at home, with friends and family that my dad's sickness would go away. I prayed to Jesus that he would wrap my dad in his arms and take away his pain. I came to understand that my prayers were answered when Dad was not sick anymore, when he rested in peace, like the thousands of others who fought their mighty battles too. No matter how angry I get at disease, and in particular this one, I know that the human spirit cannot be broken by it. I know now, after seeing the love shared by our friends and neighbors, that cancer has lost. My dad joins the ranks of so many others who won – they tied knots of love. I know that the doctors and nurses at Oneida Healthcare made us feel comfortable, courageous, and together. I couldn't ask for anything more. I know that my mom is now my hero- for just being who she is and who she made our family to be the day Dad was called heaven. She is so resilient. I can only hope to reach her level. Between the two of them, they've created a bond that was strong before, and even stronger now. I have cancer to thank for that.

When I went to print the picture, for the prayer card, I clicked on the image on my computer, and the video started unexpectedly.

You can clearly see Dad reeling in a fish, and you can hear him say, "Hank, get the net..."

I've got it, Dad.

The last return visit to New Orleans, I went to the French Market and walked my normal path. I had remembered seeing a poet at a table some years back, who had an impact on me. As I approached his table, just to the left, near the end, I saw him. I stopped and greeted him with a smile. He didn't remember me, but I glanced to his right and noticed a poem on a bookmark. It was entitled, *In My Daddy's Shoes."* I remember glancing to the middle and could make out the words, upside down. It read, "Oh to see God living in my dad each day makes me want to be like him in every single way." I looked up, and smiled again. The gentleman asked politely, "When did your Dad pass?" Shocked, I responded, "Just a month or so ago." He grinned from ear to ear. "He was in his mid-seventies, wasn't he?" I teared up and smiled again. "How did you..." He stopped me. "You need to celebrate! You had all of those great years with him. You are so fortunate. Do you want me to call your Mom?" I was again stunned. "I...I..." I stuttered.

I looked just to the right of the bookmark and there lay another: *A Mother's Love.* I picked it up, my left hand shaking. "For she will help you to run the race, and help you to learn how to gain God's grace. Many a change may come your way, this please remember on this special day." From that moment, I knew my place in my family.

Since Dad's been gone, I've come to appreciate very much one scripture in particular, Romans 8:28. It reads, "We know that all things work together for the good of those who love God; those who are called according to His purpose." It has been something that has stuck with me, and it provides understanding for me. For a kid who grew up not paying very much attention to the signs around him, this one makes it all worth while. I am not afraid anymore. I can safely accept the things around me – both good and bad. And, I believe God has called me. I know my purpose. And, it's no different from any other. Live, love, enjoy. Regardless of what happens, how it happens or why, know that God is calling you.

The next time you look up at the clouds and the sky turns into a bright sunny day…the next time you hear a baby all of a sudden stop crying and start to laugh…the next time you look at your son or daughter and know they are scared and you take away the tears…the next time you put your arm around your friend and tell her it's going to be okay…the next time you help a stranger find his way and he thanks you sincerely…the next time you come home sad, from a long terrible day and your dog lays his head on your lap...the next time you tell someone you love them and mean it more than the world...the next time you look at your reflection...remember God is standing right next to you. He heard every word.

Made in the USA
Lexington, KY
29 December 2013